KT-224-542

THE GREAT
Wok & Stir-Fry
COOKBOOK

PHOTOGRAPHY by Peter Barry

WATERCOLOUR ILLUSTRATIONS by Sally Brewer

DESIGNED by Julie Smith

EDITED by Jillian Stewart

4360
This edition published 1997 by Colour Library Direct
© 1997 CLB International, Godalming, Surrey
All rights reserved
Printed and bound in Singapore
ISBN 1-85833-639-2

THE GREAT

Wok & Stir-Fry
COOKBOOK

Colour
Library

Contents

Introduction

Food fads come and go, but one of today's most popular styles of cooking is centuries old. In the West we pride ourselves on innovative technology, but the art of stir-fry cookery, so popular today with cooks throughout Europe and America, comes from the traditional cuisine of the Orient. The essence of stir-frying is one of speed, using a simple wok to cook top quality ingredients, quickly, sealing in flavour and nutrients – it is often the case that the minimum of effort is rewarded with maximum flavour. This is an approach to cooking that perfectly suits today's rushed lifestyle, where we demand good food fast.

But as with all cooking, a successful result depends upon careful preparation and just a little understanding of what makes woks work!

Working with a Wok

A wok is the traditional cooking pot that has come to symbolise Chinese cookery. In fact the simple wok is used throughout East Asia from Korea to Indonesia, but it is with the food and flavours of Chinese cuisine that we most associate the wok. The wok has a smooth rounded shape with long sloping sides to

provide a large cooking surface so that a large quantity of food can be cooked quickly and efficiently over direct heat. Its rounded sides mean food can be stirred and tossed rapidly without being showered around the kitchen! It's a perfectly designed classic cooking utensil. Without it, stir-frying is never quite so efficient or effective. So to really master the art of stir-frying and to become adept at preparing Oriental cuisine, a wok is essential.

Choosing a wok

Traditional woks are round bottomed, making them unsuitable for use on electric or halogen hobs. Some round bottomed woks however come equipped with a stand to give stability and overcome the problem. Another alternative is to choose a wok with a flat base to sit squarely and safely directly on the hob. If you cook with a gas hob however either design is suitable. Purists would argue that the ideal would be to cook with a round bottomed wok over a gas flame so the entire wok can be moved around and shaken through the heat with one hand, while stirring and tossing the food with the other.

Holding the wok firmly while all this activity is going on, is obviously essential. Woks with one long handle are probably best, giving a firm hold not too near the heat source. These long handled types are called pau woks, while the woks with two shorter, looped handles are called Cantonese woks and are perhaps better suited for deep-frying and steaming, giving more stability. As you become more interested in Chinese cuisine you may choose to invest in more than one wok – handy also as two cooks can simultaneously bring fresh food to the table. Stir-fried food should always be served as soon as it is cooked for maximum crispness and flavour. Woks vary in size, but one with a diameter of 35.5cm/ 14 inches is ideal for use on the hob.

Caring for your wok

The traditional wok is made of carbon steel which heats up quickly, and is heavy enough for stability without being too cumbersome. Before using for the first time a steel wok must be seasoned with oil to

When the paper wipes clean your new wok is seasoned.

seal the surface, preventing food from sticking and burning and keeping rust at bay between uses.

To season a new steel wok, first clean thoroughly, scrubbing to remove any manufacturing oil (but never scrub a seasoned wok after this!) and dry. Then place the wok over a low heat and add 2 tablespoonsful of vegetable oil. Rub over the entire surface with a thick pad of kitchen paper. Continue to heat very slowly for about 10-15 minutes, then turn off the heat and rub the entire inner surface again with more folded kitchen paper. Allow the wok to cool for 5 minutes, wipe away any visible oil and repeat the coating, heating and wiping until the paper wipes clean. Your wok will gradually darken and become well seasoned the more you use it. Once seasoned, never scrub again, just wash well in plain water without any detergent and dry really thoroughly. To keep the wok free from rust, heat it gently on the hob before storing.

The seasoning process may seem tedious and it is possible to buy more modern woks which do not need the same care and attention lavished on them. However, purists claim that traditional woks, well seasoned, impart a depth of flavour to stir-fried food. More up-to-date alternatives include non-stick woks, aluminium and stainless steel woks. Electrically heated woks are also available and these control the cooking temperature evenly, although some claim that the temperature reached is not high enough for rapid stir-frying.

Wok accessories

Wok stand – traditional round bottomed woks may be sold with a ring of steel to enable the wok to sit on the hob. Not only is this essential if a round based wok is to be used on an electric hob, it is also required for gas hobs if a wok is to be used for steaming, braising or deep-frying. Stands come in two designs, one resembling a wire framework, the other a more solid ring with holes punched in it. The former framework style gives better ventilation so should be used on a gas ring to prevent a build up of fumes. Either type of stand can be used on electric hobs.

Wok ring – unlike the stand, a wok ring is used inside the wok to transform the wok into a steamer. The ring should sit inside the wok, which has water placed in the base, and a plate or bamboo steamer can then be placed clear of the water.

Bamboo steamer – these attractive bamboo baskets are almost as old as the wok itself. Made of latticework design, the slats inside the steamer allow food to be placed on them, above the steam and covered by a snug fitting lid. They can either be placed on a wok ring inside a wok or above a conventional saucepan or steamer.

Wok lid – some woks are sold complete with a domed lid. Obviously not for use in stir-frying, a lid nonetheless is handy when dishes are to be simmered or braised, as well as for steaming food when a covered bamboo steamer is not available.

Wok stirrer – a long handled stirrer is often sold with a wok to help make light work of tossing and scooping food during stir-frying. It is perfectly designed to scoop underneath ingredients and toss them over to ensure that really even cooking takes place. A long handled wooden spoon or cooking chopsticks could also be used – but do make sure the chopsticks have sufficiently long handles to keep you hands out of the wok!

The Ingredients

Stir-frying is steeped in the traditions of Chinese cuisine, a style of cooking that uses relatively large proportions of vegetables, rice and noodles to smaller quantities of meat, fish and poultry. Many stir-fry recipes keep this balance, other more contemporary dishes have a larger proportion of animal foods. All require top quality produce, carefully prepared.

Vegetables

A huge array of familiar vegetables can be successfully stir-fried. Carrots, courgettes, celery, baby corn cobs, florets of broccoli, leeks, asparagus, pepper, mange tout peas and shelled peas as well as onions, and more commonly spring onions, all feature in stir-frying. Less familiar vegetables are discussed in the glossary.

Beans, nuts and cereal grains

Vegetables are not the only plant foods to be used in stir-frying. Rice and noodles from cereal grains are often precooked (or soaked) before being finished in the wok with additional ingredients. Where would our Chinese restaurants be without chow mein or fried rice?

Rice – one of the staples of the Chinese diet, long-grain rice is used throughout Chinese recipes and is the most popular choice for all dishes, apart from the porridge-like *congee* which uses short-grain rice. White rice, rather than the easy-cook or partially cooked rice is the first choice, but the more nutritious brown rice with its richer fibre and vitamin content can be used in its place.

Noodles – in the North of China where it is too cold to grow rice, wheat forms the basic staple of the diet, many popular recipes therefore feature wheat based noodles.

Beans – the soya bean is the most widely used bean in Chinese cooking. However it is rarely found simply boiled, instead it is used in many guises to form the basis of soy sauce, varied bean pastes and sauces for flavouring, as well as in bean curd.

Nuts – almonds, peanuts, cashews, walnuts and other shelled nuts are often used in stir-frying to add a

distinctive crunchiness and flavour to food. Sometimes nuts are added at the start of cooking, being lightly cooked in the oil before being removed, set aside and then returned to the wok just before serving; this adds flavour to the oil to permeate the entire dish.

Meat, fish and poultry

Meat, fish and poultry are used in varying amounts in stir-fry dishes; but wherever they are used it is important to choose the right quality produce for a successful result.

Meat – for stir-frying the tenderest cuts are essential, offering a high proportion of lean to very little fat. Choose pork fillet, tenderloin or pork steaks; beef fillet, rump or flank steak; lamb fillet (from the neck) or lamb steaks. Some supermarkets sell pork or beef ready prepared for stir-frying – this saves time and confusion! Lambs' kidneys and liver (calves', lambs', pigs' or chicken) are also ideal for stir-frying, requiring only a short cooking time.

Poultry – chicken is highly regarded in Chinese cuisine, its mild flavour mixing well with many varied ingredients.

Requiring only a short time to tenderise, it is also ideally suited to stir-frying. Meat from the chicken breast is best; buy ready-boned breasts or remove the bone yourself by inserting a sharp knife along the breastbone and running it close against the ribs. Duck is also popular in Chinese cuisine: the classic Peking Duck is for many the ultimate dish of the country. Duck breasts are also used successfully in stir-frying.

Fish – because fish and shellfish require only a short cooking time they are tailor-made to stir-frying. The long coastline of China yields plentiful supplies from the ocean and many delicious recipes have been developed making the most of the abundance of fish. Steaming is also used for cooking fish, white fish in particular, while seafood – prawns, oysters, scallops and even lobster – is wonderful when stir-fried. Always remember that freshness is of vital importance.

These main ingredients form the basis of a vast selection of stir-fry recipes, but there are two more components of stir-fry dishes which are absolutely essential:

Oil

Only a small amount of oil is required for stir-frying, usually 1-2 tablespoonsful is sufficient, making stir-frying a lower-fat, lower-calorie method of cooking than conventional frying. However because stir-frying takes place at a high temperature care must be taken in choosing an oil that can tolerate such intensity of heat. Groundnut or peanut oil is often the first choice for cooking in a wok, being able to withstand high temperatures and having a mild taste. Corn, sunflower and soya oil can all be used satisfactorily too. Sesame oil, with its distinctive rich flavour and deep golden brown colour, tends to be added in a small quantity at the end of cooking as it does not stand up to high temperature cooking.

Flavourings

Most of the recipes in this book are Oriental in style with a distinctive flavour dimension. Adding flavourings like soy sauce, hoisin sauce and oyster sauce, and aromatics such as garlic and ginger transforms the basic foods, adding a wide range of characteristic flavours. Fresh herbs, mainly coriander, parsley, chives and the Mediterranean favourites basil, oregano and marjoram (and other fresh herbs besides), can all be used in stir-frying recipes which may have little to do with Oriental cuisine other than the fact that they are prepared in the wok! As always, freshness is vital to achieving a good flavour.

Mastering the Art of Stir-Frying

The key to successful stir-frying is to have all the ingredients required in a recipe, measured out, prepared and immediately at hand. Once the actual cooking begins the ingredients are added in rapid succession and the cooking process is short. So although the cooking time is quick, don't forget to give yourself plenty of time to fully prepare all the ingredients beforehand. There are a number of specific cutting techniques used for food that is to be stir-fried, each is designed to speed up the cooking process and to make the finished dish look attractive and appealing. Good preparation requires a sharp knife or a traditional Chinese cleaver and a stable chopping board.

Using a Chinese cleaver

If you do decide to use a Chinese cleaver get used to holding it in the correct way. Either
i) Curl your fingers tightly around the handle which should rest in the palm of your hand; see picture above, or
ii) Hold the handle in the palm of your hand as before, but slide your index finger down the side of the blade; see picture below. This allows you more control using your thumb and forefinger.

Preparing the ingredients

Straight slicing – this is the conventional method of slicing food. Hold the food firmly on the chopping board with one hand, slice straight down into very thin slices. Slice meat across the grain to help tenderise it.

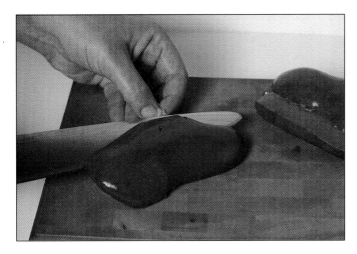

Flat or horizontal slicing – this is used to split food into two thinner pieces through the centre e.g. for slicing kidneys. Place the food on the board with the blade parallel to it. With your free hand on top to steady it, gently slice sideways through the food.

Diagonal slicing – this is often used for carrots, spring onions and asparagus for example, to expose more of the vegetable's surface for quicker cooking. Hold the food on the board and angle the blade at a slant and cut.

Roll cutting – this also exposes more of the surface of a food for speedy cooking and is ideal for thicker vegetables such as courgettes, aubergines and large carrots. Hold the food on the chopping board and make a diagonal cut at one end, rotate it 180° and make a second diagonal slice. You will have a diamond shaped chunk – now repeat this, cutting and turning along the length of the vegetable.

Shredding – this cutting technique is used for cutting bulky vegetables such as Chinese leaves, and for cutting fine matchsticks of julienne strips of other vegetables, meat or poultry, as well as the so-called silken threads of garlic. First cut the food into slices, then pile the slices on top of each other and cut them lengthways into fine strips. Shredding fresh meat or chicken breasts is easier if you first pop the meat into the freezer for 20 minutes to firm up slightly.

Dicing – rather like shredding, this process cuts food into tiny cubes or dice. First slice food, then stack several slices and cut first lengthways, then stack the strips and cut crossways into evenly sized cubes. This is used for meat, poultry or occasionally vegetables.

Other preparation techniques

Marinading – raw meat or poultry may be marinated or steeped in a soy sauce, rice wine or cornflour mixture for at least 20 minuts to tenderise it. Other flavourings such as chilli, five-spice powder, sugar or Szechuan peppercorns may also be used in the marinade to add more flavour.

Velveting – delicate foods such as fish or chicken breasts may be velveted by coating in raw egg white and cornflour and leaving to chill for 20 minutes. This coats the food helping to protect the flavour and texture during the cooking process.

Blanching – hard vegetables such as broccoli or bamboo shoots may be blanched before stir-frying to take the edge off their hardness so that stir-frying will adequately soften them without overcooking other ingredients. The food is prepared, then plunged into boiling water very briefly for 1-2 minutes.

Thickening – cornflour is widely used in stir-frying to thicken sauces and add a characteristic glaze. The cornflour must be thoroughly blended in an equal amount of cold water before being added to the wok, to prevent lumps from forming.

Garnishes

In many East Asian countries it is believed that food must please the eye as well as the taste buds and they will take great care in the presentation of dishes, all of which are usually garnished, even if only with a sprig of fresh coriander or a sprinkling of chopped coriander. Garnishing increases the enjoyment of a meal and a little extra effort combined with a few simple instructions will make all the difference to your cooking.

Spring onion 'brushes'
First trim away the top of the onion, leaving a piece about 5-7cm/2-3 inches. Trim away the root (see below).

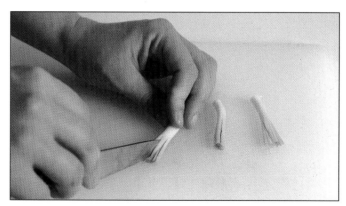

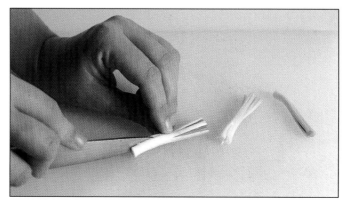

Make cuts from the green end leaving the onion joined together at the root end (centre left). Alternatively, make small cuts from both ends, not quite meeting in the middle (bottom left). Place in iced water to make the ends curl (above). When required, remove and shake off excess water. A similar effect to spring onion brushes can be achieved with chillies. For instructions on making *chilli 'flowers'* see page 48.

Chilli and spring onion curls
These are attractive scattered over a dish. Cut the stem off the chilli, trim and discard the root and top part of spring onions. Shred the chilli and spring onion lengthways. Place in iced water until curled.

The Essential Step-by-Step Guide to Stir-Frying

1. First assemble all the measured and prepared ingredients. Have ready a warmed serving dish or warmed plates. If any ingredients are first to be marinated, start this process off first, leaving yourself time to prepare the remaining ingredients.

2. Heat the empty wok over a high heat until smoke just starts to rise. This prevents the meat or fish from sticking to the surface. Add the oil, swirling it around to coat the sides.

3. If using garlic, add this now and when it starts to sizzle, add ginger, if using.

4. Add the main ingredient – meat, fish, poultry – and let each side rest for a few seconds. Slide the wok stirrer or a spoon underneath the food, turn and toss until the food is partially cooked.

5. Add any other ingredients, keeping the food moving in the wok, from the centre to the sides.

7. Add any final ingredients such as sesame oil or seeds or bean sprouts, toss briefly to combine.

6. When ready, add any sauce or cornflour mix, making a well in the centre. Stir in until the sauce has thickened and is glossy.

8. Scoop the cooked food out on the warmed dishes and serve at once. Never over-cook stir-fried food – vegetables should be tender-crisp not soft.

Glossary

Bamboo shoots – these are the young edible shoots of certain kinds of bamboo, sold canned in supermarkets and Oriental  food stores. They are a creamy yellow colour and still retain their crunchiness. Drain and rinse thoroughly before using. Any excess can be stored in a covered jar of water for up to 2 weeks in the refrigerator, so long as the water is changed daily.

Bean curd – also known as tofu, is made from a mixture of finely ground soya beans and water. As tofu, it has become much more widely available in Britain in recent years as vegetarian cookery has increased in popularity. Tofu can be bought from health food shops, Oriental food stores and some supermarkets, either fresh from the chill cabinet or processed in long-life cartons on the shelves. For stir-frying it is cut into cubes, and because it has a bland flavour, it blends well with many varied ingredients, boosting the protein value of recipes without piling on the calories.

Bean sauces – yellow bean sauce is a fermented, spicy sauce made from yellow soya beans, either sold as a sauce or as mashed beans. Black beans in sauce are small black soya beans which are also fermented to give a distinctive, slightly salty taste. Chilli bean sauce is a hot spicy mixture of soya beans, chillies and other seasonings.

Bean sprouts – most supermarkets and many good greengrocers sell fresh bean sprouts. Although all types of beans and lentils can be sprouted, most stir-fry recipes specify mung bean sprouts as they quickly form long, lean, straight shoots which add a light crunchiness to recipes.

Chillies – green chillies are hotter than red chillies of the same size and, generally speaking the smaller the chilli the hotter it is. The hottest part of the chilli is the seeds, so these should be removed for a milder flavour. Handle chillies with great care as their juice is a very strong irritant.

Chinese leaves – also known as Chinese cabbage or Peking cabbage, this is rather like an elongated white cabbage with a milder flavour and lighter textured crinkly leaves. Shred and serve raw in salads or cooked in stir-fries. It is grown on the Continent and readily available in greengrocers and supermarkets.

Coriander – fresh coriander is used in many Asian cuisines. The leaves and stems have a strong, sweetish aroma which add flavour to many dishes. The leaves are often used to garnish a dish either whole or chopped and scattered over the top. Coriander seeds are also used dry as a spice.

Five-spice powder – this is a popular flavouring mixture of five Oriental spices – star anise, Szechuan peppercorns, fennel, cloves and cinnamon.

Garlic – no stranger to the British, garlic is extensively used in stir-fry dishes either sliced, chopped or crushed and may also be used to flavour oil.

Ginger – another familiar ingredient, root ginger is an important ingredient in Oriental cuisine, where it is used chopped or sliced.

Hoisin sauce – a widely used, sweet spicy sauce, mostly associated with dishes from Southern China, especially Peking Duck. Hoisin sauce may also be sold as Chinese barbecue sauce. It is a thick dark brown sauce made from soya beans, vinegar, spices, sugar and other flavours.

Mooli – also known as daikon or white radish, mooli looks like an elongated, white parsnip. It can be steamed or boiled and served as a side dish or added to stir-fries.

Mushrooms – there are many varieties of mushrooms used in Oriental cuisine. Supermarkets and  greengrocers are now stocking a wide selection of fresh mushrooms. Of these, oyster and shiitake mushrooms are often used in stir-fry recipes, giving a fuller flavour than the conventional cultivated button, open or flat mushrooms with which we are so familiar. Dried Chinese mushrooms are also widely used in stir-fries and these can be bought in Oriental food stores or from some supermarkets. They add a distinctive flavour and aroma to many Chinese recipes. Black or brown in colour, the most highly prized are large, lightly coloured and with a cracked surface. To use Chinese dried mushrooms, soak the required amount in hot water for about 25 minutes or until they are soft. Squeeze out any excess liquid, remove the tough inedible stems and use as required. Dried cloud ears are soaked in a similar way, but rinse carefully to remove any debris, then pinch off the hard stem at the base of the 'lobes', pat with kitchen paper to remove any excess moisture and use as required. Straw mushrooms are also much loved by the Chinese, with a deep, brown cap, these are only available canned.

 *Noodles* – these are made rather like Italian pasta from a flour and water dough. If egg is added to the dough, the noodles are sold as *egg noodles*; these are

widely available from supermarkets. They require a quick 3-4 minute cooking in boiling water, keeping them fresh in cold water for use in stir-frying. *Rice noodles* are also available, made from rice flour. Much finer and white in appearance they require a short soaking in hot water before being used. Finer still are cellophane or bean thread noodles which are made from ground mung beans; like rice noodles they require only a short soaking before being ready to use.

Oyster sauce – this has a rich flavour without tasting fishy! It is made from oysters, soy sauce and brine giving a thick brown sauce used both in stir-frying and as a condiment.

Pak choi – this has smaller, darker leaves than Chinese leaves, and has broad ribbed leaf stalks rather like celery. Pak choi can be served steamed 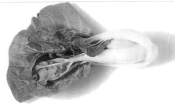 as a side dish as well as being used in stir-fries.

Rice wine – made from rice, yeast and spring water and used both for cooking and drinking, rice wine can be bought in Chinese supermarkets. Pale, dry sherry can be successfully used in its place.

Salted black beans – these are fermented, salted soya beans. Sold in small plastic bags in Oriental food stores they will keep well if transferred to an airtight jar. Wash and dry the beans prior to using and crush or chop them before adding to a dish. If unavailable, a little black bean sauce can be used as a substitute.

Soy sauce – made from a fermented mix of soya beans, flour and water, the end result is widely used. Light soy sauce tends to be used for stir-frying, whereas the thicker, richer dark soy sauce is used mostly for stews or as a dipping sauce.

Spring onions – often used as a garnish and to impart their mild onion flavour to a dish.

Spring roll wrappers – available frozen from Oriental food stores. Keep well wrapped when storing or using as they quickly dry out. Filo pastry can be used as a substitute for fried dishes.

Star anise – these star-shaped brown seed pods have a strong aniseed flavour and are widely used in Chinese and Thai cuisine. This spice is available whole or ground in some large supermarkets as well as Oriental food stores. If unobtainable, use fennel seeds as a substitute.

Szechuan pepper – this pepper is not a type of peppercorn, but the dried, reddish-brown berries of the prickly ash tree. It is not as hot as black pepper, however, it has a strong flavour and too much can temporarily numb the mouth. It is used in Szechuan cooking, which, unlike the rest of the Chinese cuisine, is extremely hot and spicy.

Turmeric – used to add colour to some dishes, it must be added sparingly due both to its startling yellow colour and slightly bitter flavour.

Water chestnuts – these are not related to the chestnuts we eat at Christmas but are white and crunchy. Some specialist shops may sell fresh water chestnuts, otherwise buy canned, draining and rinsing well and storing any unused in the fridge for up to 2 weeks.

Wonton wrappers – also known as wonton skins, these are made from the same wheat flour and egg dough that is used to make egg noodles. The dough is rolled out wafer thin and cut into squares. They are available fresh or frozen from Oriental food stores and, like spring roll wrappers, should be kept covered when using to prevent them from drying out.

Chapter 1
Soups & Starters

WONTON SOUP

Probably the best-known Chinese soup, this recipe uses
pre-made wonton wrappers for ease of preparation.

SERVES 6-8

90g/3oz finely minced chicken or pork
2 tbsps chopped fresh coriander
3 spring onions, finely chopped
2.5cm/1-inch piece fresh root ginger, peeled and
   grated
20-24 wonton wrappers
1 egg, lightly beaten
1.4 litres/2½ pints chicken stock
1 tbsp dark soy sauce
Dash of sesame oil
Salt and pepper
Fresh coriander or watercress for garnish

1. Mix together the chicken or pork, chopped
coriander, spring onions and ginger.

2. Place all the wonton wrappers on a large, flat
surface, and brush the edges of the wrappers lightly
with the beaten egg.

3. Place a small mound of filling mixture, to the side of

Step 2 Place the
wonton wrappers out
on a clean surface.
Brush the edges with
beaten egg.

Step 3 Place a
spoonful of filling on
each wonton
wrapper, to one side
of the centre.

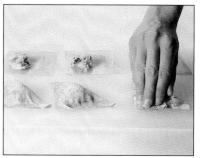

Step 3 Fold over the
tops and press firmly
together with the
fingers to seal.

the centre, on each of the wrappers and fold the other
half over the top to form a triangle. Press the edges
together with the fingers to seal well.

4. Bring the stock to the boil in a large wok. Add the
filled wontons and simmer for 5-10 minutes or until they
float to the surface. Add remaining ingredients to the
soup, using only the leaves of the coriander or
watercress for garnish.

Cook's Notes

⏱ Time
Preparation takes 25-30
minutes and cooking takes about
5-10 minutes.

Variation
Use equal quantities of
crabmeat or prawns to fill the
wontons instead of chicken or pork.

Buying Guide
Wonton wrappers are
sometimes called wonton skins.
They are available in speciality
shops, delicatessens and Chinese
supermarkets.

SPICED FRIED SOUP

Spicy and fragrant, this warming Indonesian soup is a meal in itself.

SERVES 4

About 90ml/6 tbsps oil
1 clove garlic, peeled but left whole
460g/1lb chicken breast, skinned, boned and cut into small pieces
1 cake tofu, drained and cut into 2.5cm/1-inch cubes
60g/2oz raw cashew nuts
4 shallots, roughly chopped
1 carrot, very thinly sliced
90g/3oz mange tout peas
60g/2oz Chinese noodles, soaked for 5 minutes in hot water and drained thoroughly
1.4 litres/2½ pints vegetable or chicken stock
Juice of 1 lime
¼ tsp turmeric
2 curry leaves
1 tsp grated fresh root ginger
1 tbsp soy sauce
Salt and pepper

1. Heat 2 tbsps of the oil in a wok, add the garlic and cook until brown. Remove the garlic from the wok and discard.

Step 2 Stir the chicken pieces into the hot oil, and stir-fry them until they begin to brown.

2. Add the chicken pieces and stir-fry in the oil until they begin to brown. Remove from the wok and drain well.

3. Add a little more oil to the wok and add the tofu. Stir-fry until lightly browned. Remove and drain well.

4. Add the cashews and cook, stirring constantly until toasted. Remove and drain well.

Step 6 Fry the noodles on one side until they have browned. Turn them over to brown the other side.

5. Add a little more oil and stir-fry the shallots and carrot until lightly browned. Stir in the mange tout peas and cook for 1 minute. Remove from the wok and drain.

6. Add another 2 tbsps of oil to the wok and heat until it is very hot. Add the noodles and cook quickly until brown on one side. Turn over and brown the other side.

7. Lower the heat and pour in the stock. Stir in the lime juice, turmeric, curry leaves, ginger, soy sauce and seasoning. Cover and simmer gently for 10 minutes, stirring occasionally to prevent the noodles from sticking.

8. Add the fried ingredients and heat through for 5 minutes. Serve immediately.

Cook's Notes

Time
Preparation takes about 20 minutes and cooking takes 20-25 minutes.

Variation
Substitute 225g/8oz mushrooms and 120g/4oz shredded Chinese leaves in place of the chicken, to make a delicious vegetarian meal.

Cook's Tip
If it is not possible to buy raw cashew nuts, use unsalted roasted cashew nuts, and do not fry them in the oil. If they are only available salted, rinse and dry them before using.

PEKING-STYLE SOUP

Duck stock is the base of this tasty, filling soup, which
is delicately flavoured with sesame seeds and soy sauce.

SERVES 4

4 slices smoked ham
340g/12oz Chinese leaves
700ml/1¼ pints duck stock
1 tbsp sesame seeds
Pinch of chopped garlic
1 tbsp soy sauce
½ tsp white wine vinegar
Salt and pepper
1 egg yolk, beaten

Step 1 Cut the ham into small even-sized cubes.

1. Cut the ham into small, even-sized cubes, and cut the Chinese leaves into thin shreds.

2. Heat the duck stock in a wok, add the Chinese leaves and simmer briskly for 10 minutes.

3. Stir in the sesame seeds, garlic, ham, soy sauce, vinegar and salt and pepper to taste.

4. Cook for 10 minutes over a gentle heat. Using a teaspoon, drizzle the beaten egg yolk into the soup. Serve immediately.

Cook's Notes

Time
Preparation takes about 5 minutes and cooking takes about 20 minutes.

Cook's Tip
To allow the egg yolk to drizzle into the soup in thin strands, make a hole in the bottom of a plastic or paper cup and pour in the egg yolk. Move the cup in circles over the wok.

Variation
Replace the smoked ham with a different smoked meat.

TURKEY SOUP WITH BLACK MUSHROOMS

This unusual blend of flavours makes a tasty, warming soup.

SERVES 4

175g/6oz turkey breast
1 tbsp sesame oil
60g/2oz dried black Chinese mushrooms, soaked for
    15 minutes in warm water
700ml/1¼ pints chicken stock
1 tbsp soy sauce
1 slice fresh root ginger
Salt and pepper

1. Cut the turkey meat into slices and then into small cubes.

2. Heat the sesame oil in a wok, add the turkey and stir-fry until brown. Remove from the pan and drain off all the excess oil.

3. Cook the mushrooms in boiling, salted water for 10 minutes. Rinse and drain well.

4. Place the mushrooms in the wok with the chicken stock. Stir in the meat, soy sauce, ginger and salt and pepper to taste. Bring to the boil and then cover and simmer gently for 15 minutes.

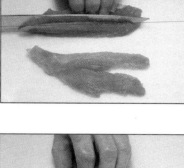

Step 1 Cut the turkey across the grain into slices.

Step 1 Cut the sliced turkey meat into small cubes.

Cook's Notes

Time
Preparation takes about 10 minutes and cooking takes about 35 minutes.

Serving Idea
Sprinkle the soup with 1 tbsp chopped fresh chives before serving.

Watchpoint
Don't forget to remove the slice of ginger before serving.

CHICKEN AND SWEETCORN SOUP

The addition of baby corn cobs to this soup makes it particularly attractive.

SERVES 4

175g/6oz canned sweetcorn
700ml/1¼ pints chicken stock
2 chicken breasts, cooked
12 baby corn cobs
2.5cm/1-inch piece of fresh root ginger, chopped
2 tbsps light soy sauce
Pinch of monosodium glutamate (optional)
Few drops of chilli sauce
Salt and pepper

Step 2 Strain the sweetcorn purée through a sieve, pushing it through with the help of a spoon.

1. Place the canned sweetcorn in a food processor with 120ml/4 fl oz of the chicken stock. Process until smooth.

2. Strain the purée through a sieve, pushing it through with the help of a spoon.

3. Cut the chicken into thin slices and stir them into the remaining stock, in a wok. Stir in the sweetcorn purée.

4. Add the baby corn and bring to the boil. Simmer for 15 minutes. Add the ginger, soy sauce, and monosodium glutamate. Continue cooking for another 10 minutes.

5. Add a few drops of chilli sauce. Check the seasoning, adding salt and pepper if necessary, and serve.

Cook's Notes

Time
Preparation takes about 5 minutes and cooking takes about 25 minutes.

Cook's Tip
Prepare the soup the day before serving to give the flavours time to develop.

Variation
Creamed sweetcorn can be used instead of the sweetcorn niblets.

SEAFOOD TEMPURA

This is a traditional Japanese dish, which can be served as an unusual starter.

SERVES 4

90ml/6 tbsps soy sauce
Finely grated rind and juice of 2 limes
60ml/4 tbsps dry sherry
12 raw king prawns
2 medium white fish fillets, skinned and cut into
    5x2cm/2x¾-inch strips
Small whole fish, e.g. smelt or whitebait
2 squid, cleaned and cut into strips 2.5x7.5cm/
    1x3 inches long
2 tbsps plain flour, for dusting
1 egg yolk
225ml/8 fl oz iced water
120g/4oz plain flour
Oil for deep-frying

1. Mix together the soy sauce, lime juice and rind, and sherry to serve as a dip with the seafood.

2. Shell the prawns, leaving the tails intact. Wash the fish and the squid and pat dry. Dust them all with the 2 tbsps flour.

Step 5 Do not batter too many pieces of fish at a time. Only coat those you are about to cook.

3. Make a batter by beating together the egg yolk and water. Sieve in the 120g/4oz of plain flour and mix in lightly with a table knife. The batter should be lumpy and under mixed.

4. Heat the oil in a wok to 180°C/350°F.

5. Dip a few pieces of seafood into the batter, shaking off any excess. Lower the pieces into the hot oil and cook for 2-3 minutes. Lift them out carefully and drain on absorbent kitchen paper, keeping warm until serving. Accompany the seafood with the dipping sauce.

Step 3 The batter will be lumpy and look under mixed.

Step 5 Cook only 3 or 4 pieces and only one kind of seafood at a time.

Cook's Notes

Time
Preparation takes about 30 minutes and cooking time varies from 2-3 minutes per batch, depending on the type of seafood.

Cook's Tip
If the batter seems to drain off too quickly, leave each batch of seafood in the bowl of batter, until you are ready to lower them into the hot oil.

Variation
Use a few vegetables, as well as seafood, for an interesting change. Whole button mushrooms are especially good.

CANTONESE EGG FU YUNG

As the name suggests, this dish is from Canton. However, fu yung dishes are popular in many other regions of China, too.

SERVES 2-3

5 eggs
60g/2oz shredded cooked meat, poultry or fish
1 stick celery, finely shredded
4 dried Chinese mushrooms, soaked in boiling water
  for 5 minutes
60g/2oz canned bean sprouts
1 small onion, thinly sliced
Pinch of salt and pepper
1 tsp dry sherry
Oil for frying

Sauce
1 tbsp cornflour dissolved in 3 tbsps cold water
280ml/½ pint chicken stock
1 tsp tomato ketchup
1 tbsp soy sauce
Pinch of salt and pepper
Dash of sesame oil

1. Beat the eggs lightly and add the shredded meat and celery.

2. Squeeze all the liquid from the dried mushrooms. Remove the stems and cut the caps into thin slices. Add to the egg mixture along with the bean sprouts and onion. Add a pinch of salt and pepper and the sherry and stir well.

3. Heat a wok and pour in about 60ml/4 tbsps oil. When hot, carefully spoon in about 90ml/3 fl oz of the egg mixture.

Step 3 Heat the oil in a wok and spoon in some egg mixture to form a patty.

4. Brown on one side, turn gently over and brown the other side. Remove the cooked patty to a plate and continue until all the mixture is cooked.

5. Combine all the sauce ingredients in a small, heavy-based pan and bring slowly to the boil, stirring continuously until thickened and cleared. Pour the sauce over the Egg Fu Yung to serve.

Step 5 Bring the sauce ingredients to the boil and cook until thick and clear.

Cook's Notes

 Time
Preparation takes 25 minutes, cooking takes about 5 minutes for the patties and 8 minutes for the sauce.

Cook's Tip
If using fresh bean sprouts, blanch in boiling water for 1 minute before using.

Variation
Use cooked shellfish such as crab, prawns or lobster, if wished. Fresh mushrooms may be used instead of the dried ones. Divide the mixture in half or in thirds and cook one large patty per person.

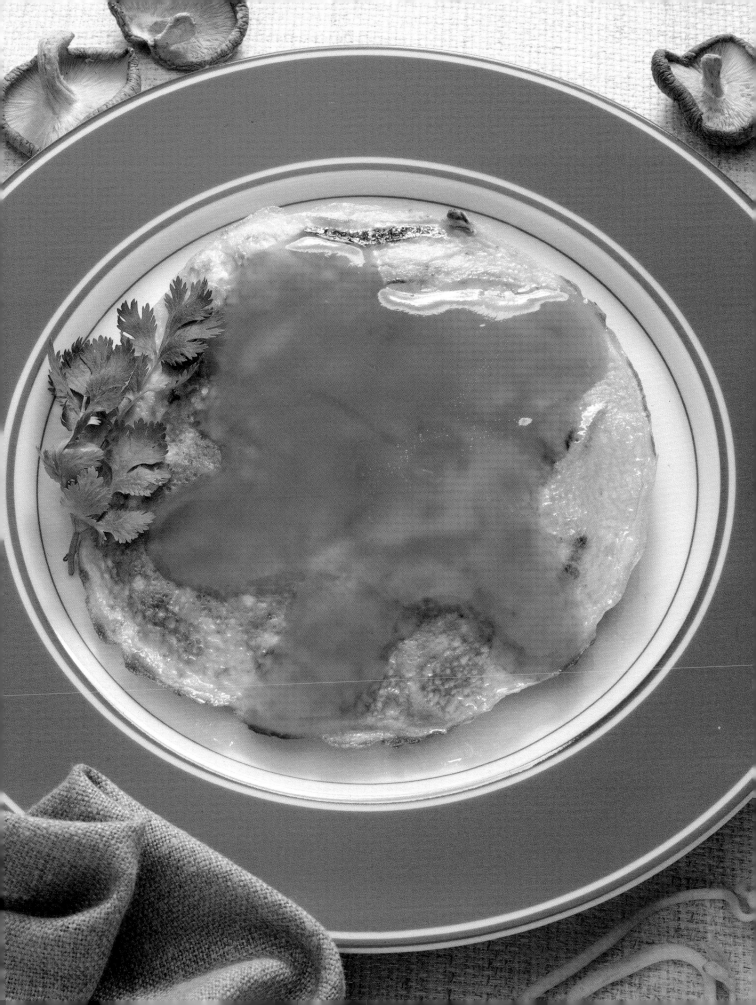

SPRING ROLLS

One of the most popular Chinese snack foods, these are
delicious dipped in sweet-and-sour sauce or plum sauce.

MAKES 12

Wrappers
120g/4oz strong plain flour
1 egg, beaten
Cold water

Filling
225g/8oz pork, trimmed and finely shredded
120g/4oz prawns, peeled and chopped
4 spring onions, finely chopped
2 tsps chopped fresh root ginger
120g/4oz Chinese leaves, shredded
100g/3½oz can bean sprouts, drained
1 tbsp light soy sauce
Dash of sesame oil

1 egg, beaten
Oil for deep-frying

1. To prepare the wrappers, sift the flour into a bowl
and make a well in the centre. Add the beaten egg and
about 1 tbsp cold water. Begin beating with a wooden
spoon, gradually drawing in the flour from the outside to
make a smooth dough. Add more water if necessary.

2. Knead the dough until elastic and pliable. Place in a
bowl, cover and chill for at least 4 hours or overnight.

3. When ready to roll out, allow the dough to come
back to room temperature. Flour a large work surface
well and roll the dough out to about 5mm/¼-inch thick.

4. Cut the dough into 12 equal squares then roll out

each until about 15cm/6 inches square. The dough
should be very thin. Cover while preparing the filling.

5. Cook the pork in a little of the frying oil for about 2-3
minutes. Add the remaining filling ingredients, cook for
a further 2-3 minutes and allow to cool.

6. Lay out the wrappers on a clean work surface with a
corner of each wrapper facing you. Brush the edges
lightly with the beaten egg.

7. Divide the filling among the dough, placing it just
above the front point. Fold the sides in like an envelope.

8. Fold over the point until the filling is completely
covered, and roll up as for a Swiss roll. Press all the
edges together to seal well.

9. Heat the oil in a large wok to 190°C/375°F. Add
2-4 spring rolls and fry until golden brown on both sides.
The rolls will float to the surface when one side has
browned and should be turned over. Drain thoroughly
on kitchen paper and serve hot.

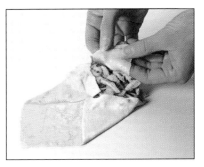

Step 7 Fill the
dough and fold the
sides like an
envelope before
rolling up.

Cook's Notes

Time
Preparation takes about 50
minutes, plus at least 4 hours
refrigeration. Cooking takes about 20
minutes.

Cook's Tip
Ready-made fresh and frozen
wrappers can be obtained from
Chinese supermarkets.

Freezing
The rolls may be frozen uncooked.
Line a baking sheet with clingfilm, place
on the rolls and freeze until nearly solid.
Wrap individually and freeze for up to
2 months. Defrost completely before
frying.

QUICK FRIED PRAWNS

Prepared with either raw or cooked prawns, this is an incredibly delicious starter that is extremely easy to cook.

SERVES 4-6

900g/2lbs cooked prawns in their shells
2 cloves garlic, crushed
2.5cm/1-inch piece fresh root ginger, finely chopped
1 tbsp chopped fresh coriander
3 tbsps oil
1 tbsp rice wine or dry sherry
1½ tbsps light soy sauce
Spring onions to garnish

Step 1 Peel the shells from the prawns, leaving only the tail ends on.

Step 1 Carefully pull the head of the prawn away from the body.

1. Shell the prawns except for the very tail ends. Place the prawns in a bowl with the remaining ingredients, except for the garnish, and leave to marinate for 30 minutes.

2. Heat a wok and add the prawns and their marinade. Stir-fry briefly to heat the prawns through.

3. Chop the spring onions roughly or cut into neat rounds. Sprinkle over the prawns to serve.

Cook's Notes

Time
Preparation takes about 15 minutes, plus 30 minutes for the prawns to marinate. Cooking takes about 2 minutes.

Watchpoint
Do not overcook the prawns as they will toughen.

Variation
If uncooked prawns are available, stir-fry with their marinade until they turn pink.

SESAME CHICKEN WINGS

This is an economical starter that is also good as a
cocktail snack or as a light meal with stir-fried vegetables.

SERVES 4-6

12 chicken wings
1 tbsp salted black beans
1 tbsp water
1 tbsp oil
2 cloves garlic, crushed
2 slices fresh root ginger, cut into fine shreds
3 tbsps soy sauce
1½ tbsps rice wine or dry sherry
Large pinch of black pepper
1 tbsp sesame seeds
Spring onions or coriander to garnish

1. Cut off and discard the wing tips. Cut between the joint to separate the wing into two pieces.

Step 1 Use a knife or kitchen scissors to cut through thick joint and separate the wing into two pieces.

Step 3 Stir-fry the garlic and ginger briefly, add the chicken wings and cook, stirring, until lightly browned.

2. Crush the beans and add the water. Leave to stand.

3. Heat the oil in a wok and add the garlic and ginger. Stir-fry briefly and add the chicken wings. Cook for about 3 minutes, stir-frying until lightly browned. Add the soy sauce and wine and stir-fry for another 30 seconds. Add the soaked black beans and black pepper.

4. Cover the wok tightly and allow to simmer for about 8-10 minutes. Uncover and turn the heat to high. Continue cooking, stirring until the liquid is almost evaporated and the chicken wings are glazed with sauce. Remove from the heat and sprinkle on the sesame seeds. Stir to coat completely and serve. Garnish with spring onions or fresh coriander, if wished.

Cook's Notes

Time
Preparation takes about 25 minutes, cooking takes about 13-14 minutes.

Watchpoint
The sesame seeds will pop slightly as they cook.

Cook's Tip
You can prepare the chicken wings ahead of time and reheat them. They are best reheated in the oven for about 10 minutes at 180°C/350°F/Gas Mark 4.

Serving Idea
To garnish with spring onion 'brushes', trim the roots and green tops of spring onions and cut both ends into thin strips, leaving the middle intact. Place in iced water for several hours or overnight for the cut ends to curl up. Drain and use as a garnish.

LAMBS' KIDNEYS WITH ASPARAGUS

Gently fried lambs' kidneys cooked in a sweet, spicy sauce and served
with asparagus tips makes an unusual and impressive starter for a dinner party.

SERVES 4

Step 2 Cut the kidneys in half, cutting out the cores.

120g/4oz small dried black Chinese mushrooms,
    soaked for 15 minutes in warm water
4 even-sized lambs' kidneys
Salt and pepper
12 green asparagus spears
2 tbsps oil
1 shallot, chopped
1 tsp dark soy sauce
1 tbsp hoisin sauce
200ml/7 fl oz chicken stock
Few drops of chilli sauce

1. Cook the mushrooms for about 10 minutes in a small quantity of boiling water. Rinse them in cold water and set aside to drain.

2. Cut the kidneys in half, cutting out the cores. Season with salt and pepper.

3. Peel and trim the asparagus and cook in boiling, lightly salted water for about 10-12 minutes or until just tender.

4. While the asparagus is cooking, heat the oil in a wok and cook the kidneys for about 3 minutes. Remove them and place on a tea-towel or kitchen paper to absorb all the juices.

5. Pour off any excess fat from the wok and add the shallot, soy sauce, hoisin sauce, mushrooms, stock and chilli sauce. Cook for 2 minutes.

6. Return the kidneys to the wok and cook until the sauce is slightly reduced. Adjust the seasoning, adding salt and pepper to taste.

7. Drain the asparagus and serve hot with the kidneys in their sauce.

Cook's Notes

Time
Preparation takes about 20 minutes and cooking takes about 35 minutes.

Cook's Tip
Make sure you drain the kidneys well to ensure that the juices don't run into the sauce and spoil the dish.

Variation
Use white asparagus or broccoli florets instead of green asparagus, and cook until tender.

Chapter 2
Fish & Seafood

SZECHUAN FISH

The piquant spiciness of Szechuan pepper is quite different
from that of black or white pepper. Beware, though,
too much can numb the mouth temporarily!

SERVES 6

Fresh chillies to garnish
460g/1lb white fish fillets (e.g. cod, hake)
Pinch of salt and pepper
1 egg
38g/5 tbsps flour
90ml/6 tbsps white wine
Oil for deep-frying
60g/2oz cooked ham, cut in small dice
2.5cm/1-inch piece fresh root ginger, finely diced
½-1 red or green chilli, seeded and finely diced
6 canned water chestnuts, finely diced
4 spring onions, finely chopped
3 tbsps light soy sauce
1 tsp rice wine vinegar or cider vinegar
½ tsp ground Szechuan pepper
280ml/½ pint light stock
1 tbsp cornflour blended with 2 tbsps water
2 tsps sugar

1. To prepare the garnish, choose unblemished chillies
with the stems on. Using a small, sharp knife, cut the
chillies in lengthwise strips, starting from the pointed
end.

2. Cut down to within 1.25cm/½-inch of the stem end.
Rinse out the seeds under cold running water and place
the chillies in iced water.

3. Leave the chillies to soak for at least 4 hours or
overnight until they open up like flowers.

4. Cut the fish fillets into 5cm/2-inch pieces and season
with salt and pepper. Beat the egg well and add the

Step 1 Cut the tip of
each chilli into strips.

flour and wine to make a batter.

5. Heat a wok and when hot, add enough oil to deep-
fry the fish. When the oil is hot, dredge the fish lightly
with flour and then dip into the batter. Mix the fish well.
Add a few pieces of fish at a time to the hot oil, and fry
until golden brown. Drain and proceed until all the fish
is cooked.

6. Remove all but 1 tbsp of oil from the wok and add
the ham, ginger, diced chilli, water chestnuts and spring
onions. Cook for about 1 minute and add the soy sauce,
vinegar and Szechuan pepper. Stir well and cook for a
further 1 minute. Remove the vegetables from the pan
and set them aside.

7. Add the stock to the wok and bring to the boil. When
boiling add 1 spoonful of the hot stock to the cornflour
mixture. Add the mixture back to the stock and reboil,
stirring constantly until thickened.

8. Stir in the sugar and return the fish and vegetables
to the sauce. Heat through for 30 seconds and serve
immediately.

Cook's Notes

Time
Preparation takes about 30
minutes. Chilli garnish takes at least
4 hours to soak. Cooking takes about
10 minutes.

Buying Guide
Szechuan peppercorns are
available in Chinese food stores,
some supermarkets or delicatessens.
If not available, substitute extra chilli.

Serving Idea
Serve with plain or fried rice. Do
not eat the chilli garnish.

CELLOPHANE NOODLES WITH PRAWNS

Cellophane noodles, also known as transparent noodles,
are made from mung bean flour and water.

SERVES 4

250g/9oz cellophane noodles
1 large spring onion
1 tbsp oil
24 fresh king prawns, peeled
1 tbsp Chinese rice wine
2 tbsps light soy sauce
½ tsp sugar
1 tbsp oyster sauce
60ml/2 fl oz fish stock
Few drops of sesame oil

1. Cook the noodles in boiling, salted water for 1 minute. Drain and rinse under cold water. Set aside to drain well.

2. To prepare the spring onion, slice off the roots and peel off the outer leaves before slicing the spring onion into thin rounds. Heat the oil in a wok and stir-fry the

Step 2 Remove the outer leaves of the spring onion.

Step 2 Cut the spring onion into thin slices.

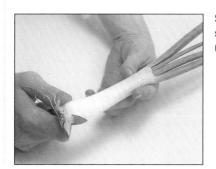

Step 2 Trim the spring onion of its roots.

spring onion and the prawns for 1 minute.

3. Reduce the heat, drain off the excess fat, and deglaze the wok with the Chinese rice wine.

4. Stir in the drained noodles, soy sauce, sugar, oyster sauce, fish stock and sesame oil.

5. Cook until the noodles are heated through and then serve immediately.

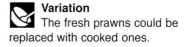

Cook's Notes

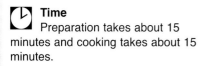

🕐 **Time**
Preparation takes about 15 minutes and cooking takes about 15 minutes.

✄ **Variation**
The fresh prawns could be replaced with cooked ones.

❗ **Watchpoint**
When adding the noodles to the wok, the heat must be reduced considerably, or the noodles will be overcooked.

SWEET-SOUR FISH

In China this dish is almost always prepared with
freshwater fish, but sea bass is also an excellent choice.

SERVES 2

1 sea bass, grey mullet or carp, weighing about
   900g/2lbs, cleaned
1 tbsp dry sherry
Few slices of fresh root ginger
120g/4oz sugar
90ml/6 tbsps cider vinegar
1 tbsp soy sauce
2 tbsps cornflour, combined with a little water
1 clove garlic, crushed
2 spring onions, shredded
1 small carrot, peeled and cut into julienne strips
30g/1oz bamboo shoots, cut into julienne strips

1. Rinse the fish well inside and out. Make three
diagonal cuts on each side of the fish with a sharp knife.
Trim off the fins, leaving the dorsal fin on top. Trim the
tail to two neat points.

2. Bring enough water to cover the fish to the boil in a
wok. Gently lower the fish into the boiling water and add
the sherry and sliced ginger. Cover the wok tightly and
remove at once from the heat. Allow to stand 15-20
minutes to let the fish cook in the residual heat.

3. To test if the fish is cooked, pull the dorsal fin – if it
comes off easily the fish is done. If not, return the wok
to the heat and bring to the boil. Remove from the heat
and leave the fish to stand a further 5 minutes.

4. Transfer the fish to a heated serving dish and keep
it warm. Remove all but 60ml/4 tbsps of the fish cooking
liquid from the wok. Add all the remaining ingredients to
the wok and cook, stirring constantly, until the sauce
thickens. Spoon some of the sauce over the fish and
serve the rest separately.

Step 1 Rinse the fish
well and make three
diagonal cuts on each
side.

Step 1 Using kitchen
scissors, trim all of
the fins except the
dorsal fin on the top.

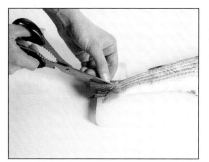

Step 1 Using kitchen
scissors again, trim
the ends of the tail to
two sharp points.

Cook's Notes

Time
Preparation takes about 25
minutes, cooking takes about 15-25
minutes.

Cook's Tip
The diagonal cuts in the side of
the fish ensure even cooking.

Variation
If wished, use smaller fish such
as trout or red mullet and shorten the
cooking time to 10-15 minutes.

KUNG PAO PRAWNS WITH CASHEW NUTS

It is said that Kung Pao invented this dish, but to this day
no one knows who he was!

SERVES 6

½ tsp chopped fresh root ginger
1 tsp chopped garlic
1½ tbsps cornflour
¼ tsp bicarbonate of soda
Salt and pepper
¼ tsp sugar
460g/1lb raw peeled prawns
60ml/4 tbsps oil
1 small onion, cut into dice
1 large or 2 small courgettes, cut into 1.25cm/½-inch
  cubes
1 small red pepper, cut into 1.25cm/½-inch squares
60g/2oz cashew nuts

Sauce
175ml/6 fl oz chicken stock
1 tbsp cornflour
2 tsps chilli sauce
2 tsps bean paste (optional)
2 tsps sesame oil
1 tbsp dry sherry or rice wine

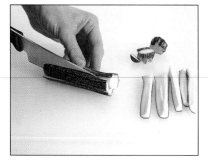

To dice the courgettes quickly, top and tail and cut into 1.25cm/½-inch strips.

Cut the strips across with a large sharp knife into 1.25cm/½-inch pieces.

1. Mix together the ginger, garlic, cornflour, bicarbonate of soda, salt and pepper and the sugar.

2. If the prawns are large, cut them in half. Add the prawns to the dry ingredients, turn to coat, and leave to stand for 20 minutes.

3. Heat the oil in a wok and when hot add the prawns. Stir-fry over a high heat for about 20 seconds, or just until the prawns change colour. Transfer to a plate.

4. Add the onion to the wok and cook for about 1 minute. Add the courgettes and red pepper and cook for about 30 seconds.

5. Mix the sauce ingredients together and add to the wok. Cook, stirring constantly, until the sauce is slightly thickened. Add the prawns and the cashew nuts and heat through completely.

Cook's Notes

Time
Preparation takes about 20 minutes, plus 20 minutes marinating. Cooking takes about 3 minutes.

Variation
If using cooked prawns, add with the vegetables. Vary the amount of chilli sauce to suit your taste.

Serving Idea
Serve with plain or fried rice.

MANGE TOUT PEAS WITH PRAWNS

Mange tout peas, peapods and snow peas are all names
for the same vegetable – bright green, crisp and edible, pods and all.

SERVES 2-4

3 tbsps oil
60g/2oz split blanched almonds, halved
120g/4oz mange tout peas
2 tsps cornflour
2 tsps light soy sauce
175ml/6 fl oz chicken stock
2 tbsps dry sherry
Salt and pepper
460g/1lb cooked, peeled prawns
60g/2oz bamboo shoots, sliced into julienne strips

1. Heat the oil in a wok. Add the almonds and cook over a moderate heat until golden brown. Remove from the oil and drain on kitchen paper.

2. To prepare the mange tout, tear off the stems and pull them downwards to remove any strings. If the mange tout are small, just remove the stalks. Add the mange tout to the hot oil and cook for about 1 minute. Remove and set aside with the almonds.

Step 2 Tear stems downward to remove strings from mange tout.

Step 2 If mange tout are very large, cut in half on the diagonal.

Step 3 Add all the ingredients to the wok and stir-fry, tossing with chopsticks or a wok stirrer.

3. Drain all the oil from the wok and mix together the cornflour and the remaining ingredients, except the prawns and bamboo shoots. Pour the mixture into the wok and stir constantly while bringing to the boil. Allow to simmer for 1-2 minutes until thickened and cleared. Stir in the prawns, bamboo shoot strips and all the other ingredients and heat through for about 1 minute. Serve immediately.

Cook's Notes

Time
Preparation takes about 10 minutes, cooking takes 6-8 minutes.

Variation
Add spring onions, celery or water chestnuts and cook with the mange tout.

Watchpoint
Do not cook the prawns too long or on heat that is too high – they toughen quite easily.

COCONUT FRIED FISH WITH CHILLIES

A real treat for lovers of spicy food.

SERVES 4

Oil for frying
460g/1lb sole or plaice fillets, skinned and cut into
    2.5cm/1-inch strips
Seasoned flour
1 egg, beaten
60g/2oz desiccated coconut
1 tsp grated fresh root ginger
1 red chilli, seeded and finely chopped
¼ tsp chilli powder
1 tsp ground coriander
½ tsp ground nutmeg
1 clove garlic, crushed
2 tbsps tomato purée
2 tbsps tomato chutney
2 tbsps dark soy sauce
2 tbsps lemon juice
2 tbsps water
1 tsp brown sugar
Salt and pepper

1. In a wok, heat about 5cm/2 inches of oil to 190°C/375°F. Toss the fish strips in the seasoned flour and then dip them into the beaten egg. Roll them in the desiccated coconut and shake off the excess.

2. Fry the fish, a few pieces at a time, in the hot oil and drain them on absorbent kitchen paper. Keep warm.

Step 1 Toss the strips of fish in the flour and then dip them in the beaten egg. Roll the fish in the desiccated coconut.

3. Remove all but 1 tbsp oil from the wok and reheat it. Add the ginger, red chilli, spices and garlic and stir-fry for about 2 minutes.

4. Add the remaining ingredients to the wok and simmer for about 3 minutes. Serve the fish, with the sauce handed round separately.

Step 2 Fry the fish in the hot oil, a few pieces at a time, to prevent it from breaking up.

Cook's Notes

Time
Preparation takes about 30 minutes and cooking takes about 20 minutes.

Cook's Tip
Great care should be taken when preparing fresh chillies. Always wash your hands thoroughly afterwards, and avoid getting any neat juice in your eyes or mouth. Rinse with plenty of water, if you do.

Preparation
Do not coat the fish too soon before frying.

Variation
Substitute a firm-fleshed fish like haddock, or monkfish, for the plaice.

SINGAPORE FISH

The cuisine of Singapore was much influenced by that of China. In turn, the Chinese brought ingredients like curry powder into their own cuisine.

SERVES 6

460g/1lb white fish fillets
1 egg white
1 tbsp cornflour
2 tsps dry white wine
Salt and pepper
Oil for frying
1 large onion, cut into 1.25cm/½-inch thick wedges
1 tbsp mild curry powder
1 small can pineapple pieces, drained and juice
    reserved, or ½ fresh pineapple, peeled and cubed
1 small can mandarin orange segments, drained and
    juice reserved
1 tbsp cornflour
Juice of 1 lime
2 tsps sugar (optional)
1 small can sliced water chestnuts, drained

Step 1 To skin the fish, hold a filleting knife at a slight angle and use a sawing motion.

Step 1 Cut the fish into even-sized pieces about 5cm/ 2 inches.

1. Skin the fish fillets using a sharp knife. Start from the tail end and angle the knife blade towards the skin at about 45 degrees. Use a sawing action and push the fish flesh along as you go. Cut the fish into even-sized pieces – about 5cm/2 inches.

2. Mix together the egg white, cornflour, wine and some salt and pepper. Place the fish in the mixture and leave to stand while heating the oil in a wok.

3. When the oil is hot, fry a few pieces of fish at a time until light golden brown and crisp. Remove the fish to kitchen paper to drain, and continue until all the fish is cooked.

4. Remove all but 1 tbsp of the oil from the wok and add the onion. Stir-fry the onion for 1-2 minutes and add the curry powder. Cook the onion and curry powder for a further 1-2 minutes. Add the juice from the pineapple and mandarin oranges and bring to the boil.

5. Combine the cornflour and lime juice and add a spoonful of the boiling fruit juice. Return the mixture to the wok and cook until thickened – about 2 minutes. Taste and add sugar if wished. Add the fruit, water chestnuts and fried fish to the wok and stir to coat. Heat through for 1 minute and serve immediately.

Cook's Notes

Time
Preparation takes about 25 minutes, cooking takes about 10 minutes.

Variation
Chicken may be used in place of the fish and cooked in the same way. Garnish with coriander leaves if wished.

Serving Idea
Serve with plain rice, fried rice or cooked Chinese noodles.

PRAWNS WITH VEGETABLES

Prawns are ideal for stir-fry dishes as they cook very quickly.

SERVES 4

½ cucumber
225g/8oz canned bean sprouts
8 dried Chinese black mushrooms, soaked in warm
    water for 15 minutes
2 tbsps peanut oil
1 clove garlic, chopped
1 tsp sugar
1 tsp oyster sauce
1 tsp wine vinegar
Salt and pepper
1 tsp oil
20 raw prawns, peeled and deveined
2 tbsps cornflour
1 tbsp soy sauce
1 tbsp sesame oil

1. Peel the cucumber all around with a sharp knife. Cut the cucumber into sections about 5cm/2-inches long then slice into thin julienne strips.

2. Rinse and drain the bean sprouts.

3. Drain the mushrooms and cook in boiling, salted water for 15 minutes. Rinse and set aside to drain.

4. Heat the peanut oil in a wok and stir-fry the garlic, bean sprouts and mushrooms for 1 minute.

5. Add the cucumber, sugar, oyster sauce, vinegar and seasoning. Cook for 2 minutes, stirring continuously.

Step 1 Peel the cucumber all around with a sharp knife or vegetable peeler.

Step 1 Slice the cucumber into thin julienne strips.

6. Heat the oil in a frying pan. Toss the prawns in the cornflour and fry them until cooked through.

7. Transfer the vegetables to a serving platter. Top with the fried prawns. Sprinkle with soy sauce and the sesame oil just before serving.

Cook's Notes

Time
Preparation takes about 15-20 minutes, cooking takes about 10 minutes.

Cook's Tip
Before serving, the vegetables should have caramelized slightly.

Preparation
It is easiest to devein the prawns by removing the black thread from the indentation along the back of the prawns with a small, sharp knife.

STIR-FRIED LOBSTER WITH GINGER

This dish is ideal for a special occasion.

SERVES 4

2 live lobsters, each 340g/12oz in weight
1 tbsp vinegar
1 courgette
1 tbsp oil
2 tsps chopped fresh root ginger
1 tbsp oyster sauce
120ml/4 fl oz fish stock
Salt and pepper
1 tsp cornflour, combined with a little water

1. To cook the lobsters, bring a large pan of salted water to the boil, and add the vinegar. Drop in the lobsters and boil for 15 minutes. Drain and allow to cool.

2. Cut the lobsters in half lengthways, using a sharp, heavy cook's knife. Discard the head sac, gills (dead men's fingers) and the intestinal vein. Cut the meat into serving-sized pieces. Crack the claws and extract the meat.

3. Cut the courgette crossways into 2 or 3 sections, then slice thinly lengthways. Cut the slices into thin julienne strips.

4. Heat the oil in a wok and stir-fry the ginger. Add the courgette and cook until tender, but still crisp. Add the lobster and heat through.

Step 4 Add the courgette julienne to the wok and stir-fry until tender-crisp.

5. Pour in the oyster sauce and fish stock, season with salt and pepper to taste and simmer to reduce.

6. Thicken the sauce with the cornflour and water mixture, stirring continuously. Serve immediately.

Step 5 Add the oyster sauce and fish stock to the wok.

Cook's Notes

 Time
Preparation takes about 45 minutes, including cooking the lobster. Cooking takes 15 minutes.

Cook's Tip
Spiny lobster (crawfish) may be used instead of lobster.

Watchpoint
Use nutcrackers to break open the lobster claws.

PRAWNS AND GINGER

Quick and easy to prepare, this dish is really delicious.

SERVES 6

2 tbsps oil
680g/1½lbs peeled prawns
2.5cm/1-inch piece fresh root ginger, peeled and finely
  chopped
2 cloves of garlic, finely chopped
2-3 spring onions, chopped
1 leek, white part only, cut into thin strips
120g/4oz peas, shelled
175g/6oz bean sprouts
2 tbsps dark soy sauce
1 tsp sugar
Pinch of salt

1. Heat the oil in a wok and stir-fry the prawns for 2-3 minutes. Set the prawns aside.

2. Reheat the oil and add the ginger and garlic. Stir quickly, then add the spring onions, leek and peas. Stir-fry for 2-3 minutes.

3. Add the bean sprouts and prawns to the cooked vegetables. Stir in the soy sauce, sugar and salt and cook for 2 minutes. Serve immediately.

Step 2 Stir-fry the spring onions, leek and peas for 2-3 minutes.

Step 3 Cook all the ingredients together for 2 minutes before serving.

Cook's Notes

Time
Preparation takes about 10 minutes and cooking takes 7-9 minutes.

Preparation
The vegetables can be prepared in advance and kept in airtight plastic boxes in the refrigerator for up to 6 hours before needed.

Serving Idea
Serve this on its own with rice or noodles, or as part of an authentic Chinese meal.

Chapter 3
Chicken & Duck

Chicken in Hot Pepper Sauce • Duck with Onions • Lemon Chicken

Chicken and Cashew Nuts • Chicken with Cloud Ears

Duck with Oranges • Chicken with Bean Sprouts

Chicken with Walnuts and Celery • Duck in Five-Spice Sauce

Chicken Livers with Chinese Leaves and Almonds

CHICKEN IN HOT PEPPER SAUCE

Add more or less chilli sauce to this dish to suit your taste.

SERVES 4

1.4kg/3lbs boneless chicken joints
2 tbsps oil
1 tsp chopped garlic
1 red pepper, cut into thin strips
1 green pepper, cut into thin strips
1 tsp wine vinegar
1 tbsp light soy sauce
1 tsp sugar
280ml/½ pint chicken stock
1 tbsp chilli sauce
Salt and pepper

Step 1 Cut all the chicken meat into thin strips, removing the skin if wished.

1. Cut all the chicken meat into thin strips, removing the skin if wished. Heat the oil in a wok and stir-fry the garlic, chicken and the red and green peppers.

2. Pour off any excess oil and deglaze the wok with the vinegar. Stir in the soy sauce, sugar and stock.

3. Gradually stir in the chilli sauce, tasting after each addition. Season with a little salt and pepper to taste.

4. Cook until the sauce has reduced slightly. Serve piping hot.

Cook's Notes

Time
Preparation takes about 10 minutes and cooking takes about 25 minutes.

Cook's Tip
A fresh green chilli could be used instead of the chilli sauce. Seed it and chop very finely. Add sparingly to the wok and taste the sauce 1 minute after each addition: the flavour develops as the chilli is heated. Repeat the process to taste.

Serving Idea
Serve with plain boiled or steamed rice.

DUCK WITH ONIONS

The rich flavour of duck is perfectly complemented by the rice wine, soy and hoisin-based sauce in this recipe.

SERVES 4

2 tbsps oil
2 large onions, finely sliced
2 large duck breasts, cut into slices
2 tbsps Chinese rice wine
1 tbsp soy sauce
1 tbsp hoisin sauce
280ml/½ pint chicken stock
Salt and pepper

1. Heat the oil in a wok and stir-fry the onions until lightly browned. Ease the onions up the side of the wok out of the oil, to keep them warm.

2. Add the duck to the wok and stir-fry until lightly browned.

3. Pour in the Chinese rice wine. Push the onions back into the bottom of the wok, with the duck.

4. Stir in the soy sauce, hoisin sauce and the stock. Allow to cook until slightly reduced. Season with salt and pepper and serve immediately.

Step 1 Stir-fry the onions until lightly browned.

Step 2 Add the duck to the wok and stir-fry until lightly browned.

Cook's Notes

Time
Preparation takes about 15 minutes and cooking takes about 15 minutes.

Variation
If wished, a whole boned duckling can be used instead of duck breasts.

LEMON CHICKEN

This Oriental dish has a fresh-tasting lemony sauce with
dried chilli providing just the right amount of spiciness.

SERVES 4

4 chicken breasts, skinned, boned and cut into thin
  strips
2 tbsps oil
Lemon slices to garnish

Marinade
60ml/4 tbsps soy sauce
2 tsps shaohsing wine or dry sherry
Salt and pepper

Sauce
3 tbsps salted black beans
2 tbsps water
90ml/6 tbsps lemon juice
225ml/8 fl oz chicken stock
60g/4 tbsps sugar
1 tsp sesame oil
3 tbsps cornflour
2 cloves garlic, finely chopped
¼ tsp dried chilli flakes

1. Mix the chicken with the marinade ingredients, cover
and refrigerate for 30 minutes.

Step 2 Crush the black beans into the water and leave to soak.

2. To prepare the sauce, crush the black beans,
combine with the water and leave to stand until ready to
use.

3. Combine the remaining sauce ingredients in a
shallow dish.

4. Heat a wok and add the oil. Remove the chicken
from the marinade with a slotted spoon, add to the wok
and stir-fry for 3-4 minutes or until cooked through.

5. Add the marinade, soaked black beans and the
sauce mixture to the wok. Bring to the boil, stirring
continuously, and cook until slightly thickened. Garnish
with lemon slices and serve immediately.

Cook's Notes

Time
Preparation takes about 20
minutes. Cooking takes about 10
minutes.

Buying Guide
Salted black beans are available
in delicatessens and Chinese grocers.
If unavailable use bottled black bean
sauce and omit the water.

Serving Idea
Serve with either plain boiled
rice or fried rice.

CHICKEN AND CASHEW NUTS

This dish is a very popular choice in Chinese restaurants.

SERVES 4

340g/12oz chicken breast, sliced into 2.5cm/1-inch pieces
1 tbsp cornflour
1 tsp salt
1 tsp sesame oil
1 tbsp light soy sauce
½ tsp sugar
75ml/5 tbsps vegetable oil
2 spring onions, trimmed and chopped
1 small onion, diced
2.5cm/1-inch piece fresh root ginger, peeled and finely sliced
2 cloves garlic, finely sliced
90g/3oz mange tout peas
60g/2oz canned bamboo shoots, thinly sliced
120g/4oz cashew nuts
2 tsps cornflour
1 tbsp hoisin sauce
250ml/9 fl oz chicken stock

1. Coat the chicken pieces in the 1 tbsp cornflour, turning carefully to ensure they are thoroughly coated.

2. Mix together the salt, sesame oil, soy sauce and

Step 1 Carefully coat the chicken pieces with the 1 tbsp cornflour.

Step 4 Add the mange tout peas and the bamboo shoots to the stir-fried onions in the wok, and continue stir-frying for about 3 minutes.

sugar in a large mixing bowl. Add the chicken, stir to coat and leave to stand in a refrigerator for 10 minutes.

3. Heat 2 tbsps of the vegetable oil in a large wok and stir-fry the spring onions, onion, ginger and garlic for 2-3 minutes.

4. Add the mange tout peas and the bamboo shoots to the onion mixture. Stir-fry for a further 3 minutes.

5. Remove the fried vegetables, add another 1 tbsp of the oil to the wok and heat through.

6. Lift the chicken pieces out of the marinade and stir-fry these in the hot oil for 3-4 minutes, until cooked through.

7. Remove the cooked chicken pieces and clean the wok out.

8. Add the remaining oil to the wok, return the chicken and fried vegetables and stir in the cashew nuts.

9. Mix together the 2 tsps cornflour, the hoisin sauce and the chicken stock. Pour this over the chicken and vegetables in the wok and cook over a moderate heat, stirring continuously until the ingredients are heated through and the sauce has thickened.

Cook's Notes

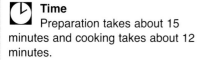

Time
Preparation takes about 15 minutes and cooking takes about 12 minutes.

Variation
Stir 90g/3oz pineapple chunks into the stir-fry mixture just before serving.

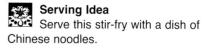

Serving Idea
Serve this stir-fry with a dish of Chinese noodles.

CHICKEN WITH CLOUD EARS

Cloud ears is the delightful name for an edible tree fungus.

SERVES 4-6

12 cloud ears, wood ears or other dried Chinese
  mushrooms
460g/1lb chicken breasts
1 egg white
2 tsps cornflour
2 tsps white wine
2 tsps sesame oil
280ml/½ pint oil for frying
2.5cm/1-inch piece fresh root ginger, peeled
1 clove garlic, peeled
280ml/½ pint chicken stock
1 tbsp cornflour
3 tbsps light soy sauce
Pinch of salt and pepper

1. Soak the dried mushrooms in boiling water for 5 minutes until they soften and swell. Remove all the skin and bone from the chicken and cut the meat into thin slices. Mix the chicken with the egg white, cornflour, wine and sesame oil.

Step 1 To swell the cloud ears or mushrooms, soak them in boiling water for 5 minutes.

Step 3 Place the chicken in the oil in small batches, and stir-fry.

2. Heat a wok for a few minutes and pour in the oil for frying. Add the whole piece of ginger and whole garlic clove to the oil and cook for about 1 minute. Take them out and reduce the heat.

3. Add about a quarter of the chicken at a time and stir-fry for about 1 minute. Remove and continue cooking until all the chicken is fried. Carefully remove all but about 2 tbsps of the oil from the wok.

4. Drain the mushrooms and squeeze them to extract all the liquid. Cut them into smaller pieces, add to the wok and cook for about 1 minute.

5. Add the stock and allow it to come almost to the boil. Mix together the cornflour and soy sauce and add a spoonful of the hot stock. Add the mixture to the wok, stirring constantly, and bring to the boil. Allow to boil for 1-2 minutes or until thickened. The sauce will clear when the cornflour has cooked sufficiently.

6. Return the chicken to the wok and add salt and pepper. Stir thoroughly for about 1 minute and serve immediately.

Cook's Notes

 Time
Preparation takes about 25 minutes, cooking takes about 5 minutes.

Preparation
When slicing the chicken, cut it across the grain as this helps it to cook more evenly. If wished, the chicken may be cut into 2.5cm/1-inch cubes.

Variation
Flat, cup or button mushrooms may be used instead of the dried mushrooms. Eliminate the soaking and slice them thickly. Add 2 tsps oyster sauce to the stock to add extra flavour.

DUCK WITH ORANGES

This traditional combination is given extra flavour by
cooking the duck in a distinctly Oriental style.

SERVES 4

3 oranges
1 duck
15g/½oz butter
1 tbsp oil
280ml/½ pint light chicken stock
90ml/6 tbsps red wine
2 tbsps redcurrant jelly
Salt and freshly ground black pepper
1 tsp arrowroot
1 tbsp cold water
Watercress to garnish (optional)

1. Using a potato peeler, carefully pare the rind thinly off 2 of the oranges.

2. Cut the rind into very fine julienne shreds using a sharp knife. Put the shredded orange rind into a small bowl and cover with boiling water. Set aside to blanch for 5 minutes, then drain.

3. Squeeze the juice from the 2 oranges. Set this aside. Cut away all the peel and the pith from the remaining

Step 2 Using a sharp knife, carefully cut the pared orange rind into very thin julienne strips.

Step 5 Cut each half of the duck into 2.5cm/1-inch strips using poultry shears or a very sharp knife.

orange and then slice the flesh into thin rounds. Set aside.

4. Wash the duck and dry well with absorbent kitchen paper. Heat the butter and the oil in a large wok. Add the duck and fry, turning frequently until it is brown all over.

5. Remove the duck from the wok, cool slightly and using poultry shears, cut away the leg and wing ends. Cut the duck in half lengthways and then cut each half into 2.5cm/1-inch strips.

6. Remove the fat from the wok and return the duck to the wok. Add the stock, red wine, redcurrant jelly, squeezed orange juice, and the well drained strips of rind. Bring to the boil, then season to taste. Reduce the heat, cover the wok and simmer the duck gently for 20 minutes, or until well cooked.

7. Skim away any surface fat and thicken the sauce by mixing the arrowroot with the water and stirring into the wok. Bring the mixture back to the boil and simmer for a further 5 minutes, or until the sauce is thick.

8. Arrange the duck on a serving plate and garnish with the orange slices and some watercress, if liked.

Cook's Notes

Time
Preparation takes 30 minutes, cooking takes 35 minutes.

Cook's Tip
When making the julienne strips, make sure there is no white pith on the back of the orange peel as this will make it bitter.

Serving Idea
Serve with plain boiled rice or sautéed potatoes.

CHICKEN WITH BEAN SPROUTS

In this recipe marinated chicken is stir-fried with bean sprouts and served with a sauce based on the marinade.

SERVES 4

1.4kg/3lbs boned chicken pieces
1 tbsp Chinese wine
1 tsp cornflour
225g/8oz fresh bean sprouts
2 tbsps oil
½ spring onion, finely sliced
1 tsp sugar
280ml/½ pint chicken stock
Salt and pepper

1. Cut the chicken into thin slices or strips. Place in a bowl and pour over the Chinese wine. Sprinkle over the cornflour and stir together well. Leave to marinate for 30 minutes.

2. Blanch the bean sprouts in boiling, lightly salted water for 1 minute. Rinse under cold running water and set aside to drain.

3. Remove the chicken from the marinade with a spoon. Heat the oil in a wok and stir-fry the chicken with the spring onion for 3-4 minutes.

4. Add the drained bean sprouts and the sugar. Stir in the marinade and the stock. Cook for 2-3 minutes.

Step 1 Cut the chicken into thin slices or strips.

Step 1 Place the chicken in a bowl and add the Chinese wine.

Check the seasoning, adding salt and pepper to taste. Serve immediately.

Cook's Notes

Time
Preparation takes about 20 minutes, plus 30 minutes marinating. Cooking takes about 10 minutes.

Cook's Tip
If using canned bean sprouts there is no need to blanch them in boiling water.

Watchpoint
As soon as you add the marinade to the wok, the mixture will thicken, so have the stock ready to pour in immediately and stir continuously until all the ingredients have been fully incorporated.

CHICKEN WITH WALNUTS AND CELERY

Oyster sauce lends a subtle, slightly salty taste to this Cantonese dish.

SERVES 2-4

225g/8oz boned chicken, cut into 2.5cm/1-inch pieces
2 tsps soy sauce
2 tsps brandy
1 tsp cornflour
Salt and pepper
2 tbsps oil
1 clove garlic
120g/4oz walnut halves
3 sticks celery, cut in diagonal slices
2 tsps oyster sauce
140ml/¼ pint chicken stock

1. Combine the chicken with the soy sauce, brandy,

Step 3 Cook the chicken until done but not brown.

Step 3 Add the walnuts to the wok and cook until they are crisp.

cornflour and salt and pepper.

2. Heat a wok and add the oil and garlic. Cook for about 1 minute to flavour the oil.

3. Remove the garlic and add the chicken in two batches. Stir-fry quickly without allowing the chicken to brown. Remove the chicken and add the walnuts to the wok. Cook for about 2 minutes until the walnuts are lightly brown and crisp.

4. Add the celery to the wok and cook for about 1 minute. Add the oyster sauce and stock and bring to the boil. When boiling, return the chicken to the wok and stir to coat all the ingredients well. Serve immediately.

Cook's Notes

Time
Preparation takes about 20 minutes and cooking takes about 8 minutes.

Watchpoint
Nuts can burn very easily. Stir them constantly for even browning.

Variation
Almonds or cashew nuts may be used instead of the walnuts. If the cashew nuts are already roasted, add them along with the celery.

DUCK IN FIVE-SPICE SAUCE

Water chestnuts and bamboo shoots add a good contrast
of texture and flavour to this rich dish.

SERVES 4

4 dried Chinese shiitake mushrooms
12 canned water chestnuts
120g/4oz canned bamboo shoots
1 tbsp sesame oil
1 tsp chopped fresh root ginger
3 duck breasts, cut into thin slices
280ml/½ pint duck stock
1 tsp five-spice powder
Salt and pepper
1 tsp cornflour, combined with a little water

1. Soak the dried mushrooms in warm water for 15

Step 2 Blanch the water chestnuts in boiling salted water for 10 minutes.

minutes. Drain them, remove the stalks and thinly slice the caps.

2. Rinse the water chestnuts and blanch in boiling, lightly salted water for 10 minutes. Lift out and set them aside to drain.

3. Blanch the bamboo shoots in the same water, rinse and then drain. Once well drained, cut them into thin matchsticks.

4. Heat the sesame oil in a wok, add the ginger and the duck slices, and stir-fry until the duck slices are sealed.

5. Remove the ginger and duck with a slotted spoon and stir-fry the bamboo shoots, chopped Chinese mushrooms and water chestnuts.

6. Pour off any excess fat and return the duck and the ginger to the wok with the previous ingredients. Add the duck stock and stir well. Sprinkle over the five-spice powder and allow to cook for about 15 minutes.

7. Check the seasoning, adding salt and pepper as necessary. Thicken the sauce by adding the cornflour mixture and bringing to the boil. Stir continuously until the required consistency is reached.

Cook's Notes

Time
Preparation takes about 25 minutes and cooking takes about 30 minutes.

Variation
If you have no duck stock, use chicken stock instead.

Buying Guide
Dried Chinese mushrooms are available from specialist food shops and Oriental supermarkets. Fresh shiitake mushrooms are sometimes available at large supermarkets.

CHICKEN LIVERS WITH CHINESE LEAVES AND ALMONDS

Chicken livers are very low in fat and high in flavour. They also require very little cooking so are perfect for stir-fry recipes.

SERVES 4

460g/1lb chicken livers
3 tbsps sesame oil
60g/2oz split blanched almonds
1 clove garlic, peeled
60g/2oz mange tout peas, trimmed
8-10 leaves Chinese cabbage, shredded
2 tsps cornflour
1 tbsp cold water
2 tbsps soy sauce
140ml/¼ pint chicken or vegetable stock

Step 1 Trim the chicken livers, cutting away any discoloured areas, bits of fat or tubes, using a sharp knife.

1. Trim the chicken livers, removing any discoloured areas or fatty tubes. Cut the livers into even-sized pieces.

2. Heat a wok and pour in the oil. When the oil is hot, reduce the heat and stir-fry the almonds until they are pale golden brown. Remove the almonds, draining any oil back into the wok, and set them aside on absorbent kitchen paper.

3. Add the whole garlic clove to the wok and cook for 1-2 minutes to flavour the oil only. Remove the clove of garlic and discard.

4. Stir the chicken livers into the flavoured oil and cook for 2-3 minutes, stirring frequently to brown evenly. Remove the chicken livers from the wok and set them aside.

5. Add the mange tout peas to the hot oil and stir-fry for 1 minute. Stir in the Chinese leaves and cook for 1 minute further. Remove the vegetables and set aside.

Step 2 Stir-fry the almonds in the hot oil until they are a pale golden brown.

6. Mix together the cornflour and water, then blend in the soy sauce and stock. Pour the mixture into the wok and bring to the boil, stirring until the sauce has thickened and cleared.

7. Return all other ingredients to the wok and heat through for 1 minute. Serve immediately.

Cook's Notes

Time
Preparation takes 25 minutes, cooking takes 5-6 minutes.

Variation
Use finely sliced lambs' or calves' liver in place of the chicken livers.

Serving Idea
Serve with fried rice or noodles.

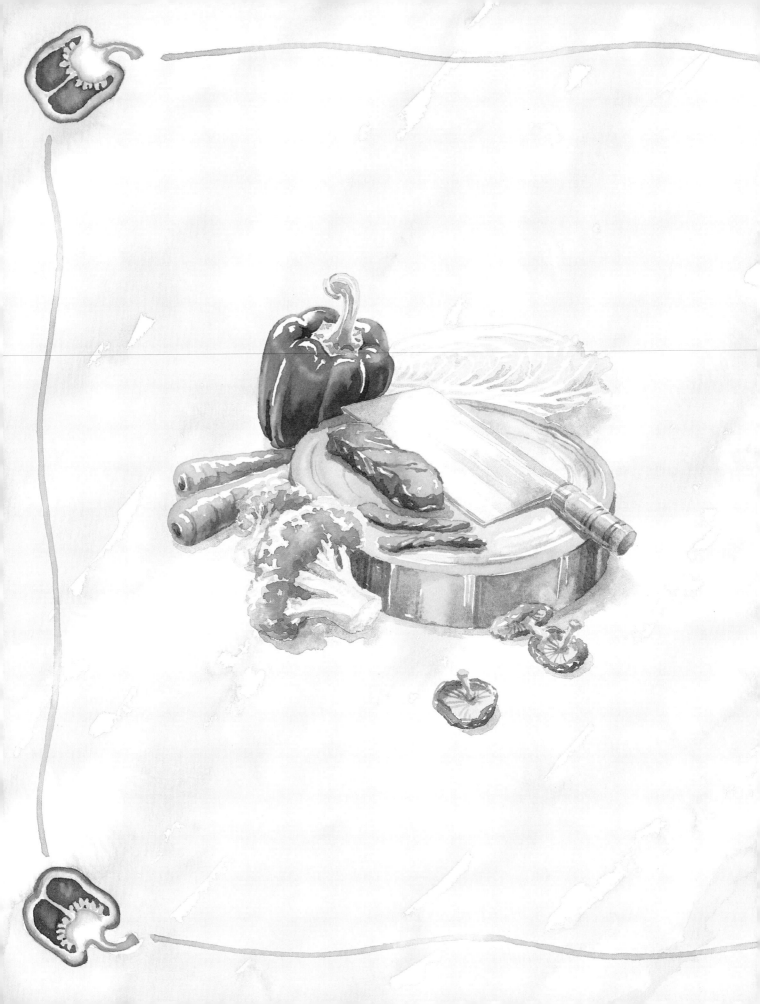

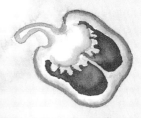

Chapter 4
Meat

Sweet and Sour Pork • Pork with Green Peppers • Pork with Bamboo Shoots

Pork and Prawn Chow Mein • Stir-Fried Pork and Vegetables

Pork Fritters • Pork in Sweet and Sour Sauce • Pork with Chinese Vegetables

Beef with Tomato and Pepper in Black Bean Sauce

Beef with Ginger Sauce • Stir-Fried Beef with Pineapple

Tomato Beef Stir-Fry • Beef in Oyster Sauce • Beef with Pineapple and Peppers

Stir-Fried Calves' Liver with Peppers and Carrots • Peking Beef

Beef with Broccoli • Shredded Beef with Vegetables • Spiced Beef

Beef with Onions • Lamb with Transparent Noodles

Stir-Fried Lamb with Sesame Seeds • Kidneys with Bacon

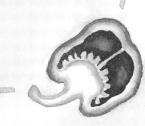

SWEET AND SOUR PORK

This really needs no introduction because of its popularity. The dish originated in Canton, but is reproduced in most of the world's Chinese restaurants.

SERVES 2-4

Batter
120g/4oz plain flour
60g/4 tbsps cornflour
1½ tsps baking powder
Pinch of salt
1 tbsp oil
Water

Oil for frying
225g/8oz pork fillet, cut into 1.25cm/½-inch cubes
1 onion, sliced
1 green pepper, sliced
1 small can pineapple chunks in natural juice, juice
  reserved

Sweet and Sour Sauce
2 tbsps cornflour
120g/4oz light soft brown sugar
Pinch of salt
120ml/4 fl oz cider vinegar or rice vinegar
1 clove garlic, crushed
1 tsp fresh root ginger, grated
90ml/6 tbsps tomato ketchup
90ml/6 tbsps reserved pineapple juice

1. To prepare the batter, sift the flour, cornflour, baking powder and salt into a bowl. Make a well in the centre and add the oil and enough water to make a thick, smooth batter. Using a wooden spoon, stir the ingredients in the well, gradually incorporating flour from the outside, and beat until smooth.

2. Heat enough oil in a wok to deep-fry the pork. Dip the pork cubes one at a time into the batter and drop into the hot oil. Fry 4-5 pieces of pork at a time and remove them with a draining spoon to kitchen paper. Continue until all the pork is fried.

3. Pour off most of the oil from the wok and add the sliced onion, pepper and pineapple. Cook over a high heat for 1-2 minutes. Remove and set aside.

4. Mix all the sweet and sour sauce ingredients together and pour into the wok. Bring slowly to the boil, stirring continuously until thickened. Allow to simmer for about 1-2 minutes or until completely clear.

5. Add the vegetables, pineapple and pork cubes to the sauce and stir to coat completely. Reheat for 1-2 minutes and serve immediately.

Step 3 Place the onion half flat on a chopping board and use a large, sharp knife to cut across into thick or thin slices as preferred. Separate these into individual strips.

Cook's Notes

Time
Preparation takes about 15 minutes, cooking takes about 15 minutes.

Cook's Tip
If the pork is prepared ahead of time it will have to be refried before serving, to crisp up.

Variation
Use beef or chicken instead of the pork. Uncooked, peeled prawns may be used as can a white-fleshed fish, cut into 2.5cm/1-inch pieces.

PORK WITH GREEN PEPPERS

This recipe is a quickly prepared, stir-fried pork dish with
green peppers and a hoisin-based sauce.

SERVES 4

460g/1lb pork fillet
2 tbsps oil
½ tsp chopped garlic
2 green peppers, cut into thin matchsticks
1 tsp wine vinegar
2 tbsps chicken stock
1 tbsp hoisin sauce
Salt and pepper
1 tsp cornflour, combined with a little water

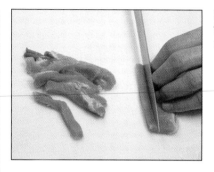

Step 1 Slice the pork thinly, then cut into narrow strips.

1. Slice the pork thinly, then cut into narrow strips. Heat the oil in a wok. Add the garlic, green pepper and the meat and stir-fry for 1 minute, shaking the wok occasionally.

2. Stir in the wine vinegar, stock and hoisin sauce. Season to taste with salt and pepper. Cook for 3 minutes.

3. Stir in the cornflour mixture and cook, stirring continuously, until the required consistency is reached.

Cook's Notes

Time
Preparation takes about 10 minutes and cooking takes 5 minutes.

Cook's Tip
Use partially frozen meat to make it easier to cut into strips. Allow the pork to completely defrost before cooking.

Variation
Use chicken breasts instead of pork, and slice thinly across the grain.

PORK WITH BAMBOO SHOOTS

Bamboo shoots and courgettes add colour and texture
to this simple pork dish.

SERVES 4

460g/1lb lean pork
Salt and pepper
225g/8oz canned bamboo shoots
1 courgette
2 tbsps oil
1 spring onion, chopped
120ml/4 fl oz chicken stock
1 tbsp soy sauce
1 tsp cornflour, combined with a little water

1. Cut the pork into very thin slices and season with salt and pepper.

2. Cut the bamboo shoots into small squares and blanch in boiling, lightly salted water for 2 minutes. Drain well.

3. Using a sharp knife, peel the courgette thickly lengthways. Discard the remaining flesh and seeds. Slice the peel thinly.

4. Heat the oil in a wok, add the spring onion and the meat. Stir-fry for 1 minute.

5. Pour off any excess fat and stir in the stock. Add the bamboo shoots and the courgette. Cook gently for 7 minutes.

Step 5 Add the stock to the meat and spring onions.

Step 5 Add the bamboo shoots and courgette and cook gently for 7 minutes.

6. Stir in the soy sauce and add the cornflour gradually, stirring continuously until the sauce has thickened. Add salt and pepper to taste. Serve hot.

Cook's Notes

Time
Preparation takes about 10 minutes and cooking takes about 15 minutes.

Cook's Tip
It is very important to blanch the bamboo shoots first to remove bitterness.

Variation
Sliced baby corn cobs could be added instead of bamboo shoots.

PORK AND PRAWN CHOW MEIN

Chinese chow mein dishes are usually based on noodles,
using more expensive ingredients in small amounts.
This makes economical everyday fare.
SERVES 4-6

225g/8oz medium dried Chinese noodles
1 small red pepper
1 carrot
2 tbsps oil
225g/8oz pork fillet, thinly sliced
90g/3oz canned bean sprouts, drained
60g/2oz mange tout peas
1 tbsp rice wine or dry sherry
2 tbsps soy sauce
120g/4oz peeled, cooked prawns

1. Cook the noodles in plenty of boiling, salted water for about 4-5 minutes. Rinse under hot water and drain thoroughly.

2. Core, seed and slice the red pepper. Peel the carrot and cut into julienne strips.

Step 1 Place whole sheets of noodles into rapidly boiling, salted water. Stir as the noodles start to soften.

Step 2 Cut the pepper in half, remove the core and seeds and slice thinly.

Step 5 Add the cooked noodles to the other ingredients in the wok and use chopsticks or a fish slice to toss over a high heat.

3. Heat a wok and add the oil. Stir-fry the pork for 4-5 minutes or until almost cooked. Add the carrot to the wok and cook for 1-2 minutes.

4. Add the remaining vegetables, wine and soy sauce to the wok and cook for about 2 minutes.

5. Add the cooked, drained noodles and prawns and toss over the heat for 1-2 minutes. Serve immediately.

Cook's Notes

Time
Preparation takes about 20 minutes. The noodles take 4-5 minutes to cook and the stir-fried ingredients need to cook for about 5-6 minutes for the pork and about 3 minutes for the vegetables.

Variation
Use green pepper instead of red, or add other vegetables such as baby corn cobs, mushrooms or peas.

Buying Guide
Dried Chinese noodles are available in three thicknesses. Thin noodles are usually reserved for soup, while medium and thick noodles are used for fried dishes.

STIR-FRIED PORK AND VEGETABLES

This recipe is a quick and easy stir-fry of pork, bean sprouts and carrot, served in a spicy, slightly sweet sauce.
SERVES 4

1 carrot, cut into thin matchsticks
225g/8oz fresh bean sprouts
2 tbsps oil
Slice of fresh root ginger
1 spring onion, chopped
½ tsp chopped garlic
460g/1lb pork, cut into thin slices
2 tsps sake
280ml/½ pint chicken stock
Salt and pepper
½ tsp brown sugar
1 tsp cornflour, combined with a little water

1. Blanch the carrot matchsticks in boiling, salted water for 1 minute. Drain well, reserving the water.

2. Wash the bean sprouts in lots of running water and

Step 4 Add the sake to the wok and allow the alcohol to evaporate before adding the stock.

blanch for 1 minute in the water used for the carrot. Rinse well and drain.

3. Heat the oil in a wok. Stir-fry the ginger, spring onion and the garlic until slightly coloured. Add the meat, stir in well and cook for 1 minute.

4. Add the well-drained vegetables, sake and stock. Season with salt and pepper, stir together well and cook for 2 minutes.

5. Using a slotted spoon, take out the meat and the vegetables and keep warm.

6. Add the sugar to the contents of the wok and thicken the sauce with the cornflour mixture, adding it gradually and stirring continuously until the required consistency is reached.

7. Remove the ginger, return the meat and vegetables to the wok and serve hot.

Step 3 Add the meat to the wok and cook for 1 minute.

Cook's Notes

Time
Preparation takes about 25 minutes and cooking takes about 10 minutes.

Variation
Use Chinese rice wine or even dry sherry if sake is unavailable.

Serving Idea
Sprinkle a few drops of sesame oil over the finished dish.

PORK FRITTERS

Thin julienne strips of lemon zest in the batter add a
delicious flavour to these pork fritters.

SERVES 4

400g/14oz pork tenderloin
2 tbsps oil
175g/6oz flour
1½ tsps baking powder
1 tsp julienned lemon zest, blanched in boiling water
1 egg, beaten
120ml/4 fl oz milk
Oil for deep-frying
Salt and pepper

Step 2 Beat in the egg and milk to form a smooth batter.

1. Cut the meat into thin slices or small cubes. Heat the

Step 2 Add the lemon zest to the flour.

oil in a wok and stir-fry the meat until almost cooked, which should take about 2 minutes. Drain and set aside.

2. Place the flour in a mixing bowl, add the baking powder and the blanched lemon zest. Beat in the egg and the milk to form a smooth batter.

3. Heat the oil for deep-frying to 180°C/350°F in the wok. Dip the slices or cubes of meat into the batter and lower into the preheated oil.

4. Fry until puffy and golden, then drain on kitchen paper. Serve hot, seasoned with salt and pepper.

Cook's Notes

Time
Preparation takes about 15 minutes and cooking, depending on how many batches you have to fry, takes about 35 minutes.

Watchpoint
Do not heat the oil over 180°C/350°F, or the batter will be done before the pork is cooked through.

Serving Idea
Serve with a dipping sauce, such as plum sauce.

PORK IN SWEET AND SOUR SAUCE

In this sweet and sour recipe the pork is simply stir-fried,
and not coated in batter.

SERVES 4

1 onion
¼ cucumber
½ red pepper
½ green pepper
1 slice pineapple, fresh or canned
60ml/4 tbsps pineapple juice
3 tbsps wine vinegar
1 tsp chilli sauce
1 tbsp sugar
½ tomato, skinned, seeded and crushed
340ml/12 fl oz chicken stock
Salt and pepper
2 tbsps oil
460g/1lb lean pork, cut into thin strips
1 clove garlic, chopped
1 tsp cornflour, mixed with 1 tsp water

1. Cut the onion, cucumber, red and green pepper and pineapple into thin matchsticks.

2. In a small bowl, mix together the pineapple juice, vinegar, chilli sauce, sugar, crushed tomato, chicken stock and some seasoning.

3. Heat the oil in a wok, stir-fry the pork and the garlic. Once the meat is golden brown, remove with a slotted spoon and set aside.

4. Add all the vegetables and the pineapple to the wok and stir-fry for 2 minutes.

Step 5 Return the pork to the wok and mix with the vegetables.

Step 5 Add the stock mixture to the wok and cook for 3-4 minutes.

5. Return the pork to the wok with the vegetables and pineapple and pour over the contents of the bowl. Cook for 3-4 minutes, stirring and shaking the wok from time to time.

6. Thicken the sauce by gradually adding the cornflour mixture, stirring continuously until the required consistency is reached. Season to taste with salt and pepper.

Cook's Notes

Time
Preparation takes about 25 minutes and cooking takes about 12 minutes.

Variation
Replace the pineapple juice with orange juice.

Watchpoint
The vegetables must be stir-fried quickly so that they remain slightly crisp.

PORK WITH CHINESE VEGETABLES

Marinated pork, stir-fried with mushrooms and bamboo shoots are delicious served in a ginger flavoured sauce.

SERVES 4

460g/1lb pork fillet
½ tsp chopped garlic
½ tsp chopped fresh root ginger
½ tsp cornflour
Few drops of chilli sauce
1 tbsp wine vinegar
1 tbsp soy sauce
225g/8oz bamboo shoots
60g/2oz dried Chinese black mushrooms, soaked for 15 minutes in warm water
2 tbsps oil
280ml/½ pint chicken stock

Step 2 Add just a few drops of chilli sauce to the marinade as it is very hot.

Step 2 Sprinkle the soy sauce over the meat and leave to marinate for 20 minutes.

Step 1 Add the ginger and garlic to the meat.

1. Cut the pork into small cubes and place in a bowl. Place the garlic and ginger on top of the cubed meat and sprinkle over the cornflour.

2. Add a few drops of chilli sauce, but not too much as it is very hot, then add the wine vinegar. Finally sprinkle over the soy sauce. Stir the meat to coat and leave to marinate for 20 minutes at room temperature.

3. Cut the bamboo shoots into thin strips, blanch them in boiling, lightly salted water, rinse in cold water and set aside to drain.

4. Rinse the soaked mushrooms and set aside to drain.

5. Remove the meat from the marinade with a slotted spoon. Reserve the marinade.

6. Heat the oil in a wok and stir-fry the meat. Pour off any excess oil and pour in the stock.

7. Stir in the mushrooms and bamboo shoots, add the marinade and cook together until thickened. Serve hot.

Cook's Notes

Time
Preparation takes about 10 minutes, plus 20 minutes marinating. Cooking takes about 10 minutes.

Cook's Tip
Since the marinade contains cornflour, the sauce will thicken when cooked. Stir continuously to prevent lumps forming.

Variation
If dried black mushrooms are unavailable, substitute ordinary fresh mushrooms – omit the soaking and just slice them.

BEEF WITH TOMATO AND PEPPER IN BLACK BEAN SAUCE

Black beans are a speciality of Cantonese cooking and give a pungent, salty taste to stir-fried dishes.

SERVES 6

2 large ripe tomatoes
2 tbsps salted black beans
2 tbsps water
60ml/4 tbsps dark soy sauce
1 tbsp cornflour
1 tbsp dry sherry
1 tsp sugar
460g/1lb rump steak, cut into thin strips
1 small green pepper
60ml/4 tbsps oil
175ml/6 fl oz beef stock
Pinch of black pepper

1. Core tomatoes and cut them into 16 wedges. Crush the black beans, combine with the water and set aside.

2. Combine the soy sauce, cornflour, sherry and sugar in a bowl. Add the meat to the marinade, stir to coat and set aside.

3. Cut the pepper into 1.25cm/½-inch diagonal pieces. Heat a wok and add the oil. When hot, stir-fry the green pepper pieces for about 1 minute and remove.

4. Add the meat and the soy sauce mixture to the wok and stir-fry for about 2 minutes. Add the soaked black

Step 1 Remove cores from the tomatoes with a sharp knife. Cut into even-sized wedges.

beans and the stock. Bring to the boil and allow to thicken slightly. Return the peppers to the wok and add the tomatoes and black pepper. Heat through for 1 minute and serve immediately.

Step 4 Add the beef mixture to the hot wok and stir-fry until liquid ingredients glaze the meat.

Cook's Notes

 Time
Preparation takes about 25 minutes, cooking takes about 5 minutes.

 Watchpoint
Do not add the tomatoes too early or stir the mixture too vigorously once they are added or they will fall apart.

Variation
Substitute mange tout peas for the green peppers in the recipe. Mushrooms can also be added and cooked with the peppers or mange tout peas.

Serving Idea
Serve with plain boiled rice.

BEEF WITH GINGER SAUCE

This dish of beef with fresh root ginger, served in a soy
and tomato sauce, is really quick to prepare and cook.

SERVES 4

460g/1lb fillet of beef
2 tbsps oil
2 tbsps fresh root ginger, peeled and cut into small
   matchsticks
2 tomatoes, skinned, seeded and finely chopped
1 tsp sugar
1 tbsp red wine vinegar
2 tbsps soy sauce
Salt and pepper

Step 4 Cook the mixture for a few minutes to allow the flavours to develop.

Step 2 Add the beef and ginger to the wok and stir-fry for 1 minute.

1. Cut the beef into very thin slices.

2. Heat the oil in a wok, add the meat and the ginger and stir-fry for 1 minute.

3. Pour off any excess fat, and stir in the tomatoes. Reduce the heat and add the sugar, vinegar and the soy sauce.

4. Cook for a few minutes to allow the flavours to develop, then season with salt and pepper to taste and serve immediately.

Cook's Notes

Time
Preparation takes about 10 minutes and cooking takes about 5 minutes.

Cook's Tip
Using partially frozen beef makes it easier to cut the meat into very thin slices. Allow the meat to finish defrosting before cooking.

Watchpoint
Do not allow the ginger to cook for too long, or its flavour will be spoiled.

STIR-FRIED BEEF WITH PINEAPPLE

In this dish, the sweet, pungent sauce complements the beef perfectly.

SERVES 4

460g/1lb fillet steak
Salt and pepper
½ fresh ripe pineapple
1 tbsp oil
1 spring onion, chopped
½ tsp chopped fresh root ginger
1 tsp vinegar
1 tsp sugar
2 tsps light soy sauce
280ml/½ pint chicken stock
120ml/4 fl oz pineapple juice
1 small tomato, seeded and chopped
1 tsp cornflour, combined with a little water

1. Cut the fillet steak into thin strips across the grain and season with salt and pepper.

2. Peel the pineapple and cut out all the brown 'eyes' from the flesh. Cut into round slices, removing any tough parts and the core. Cut the flesh into small, even pieces.

3. Heat the oil in a wok. Add the spring onion, ginger and the meat and stir-fry until lightly coloured. Pour off any excess fat.

4. Stir in the vinegar, sugar, soy sauce, chicken stock and pineapple juice. Add the tomato and the pineapple pieces, reduce the heat and cook for a few minutes.

5. Add the cornflour mixture gradually to the wok, stirring continuously until the required consistency is reached.

Step 2 Cut the top off the pineapple and peel the pineapple with a sharp knife.

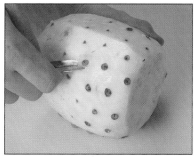

Step 2 Cut out all the brown 'eyes' using the end of a vegetable peeler.

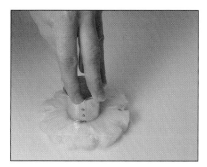

Step 2 Cut the core out from the centre of the pineapple slices.

Cook's Notes

Time
Preparation takes about 15 minutes and cooking takes about 10 minutes.

Variation
Instead of buying pineapple juice, liquidise the remaining ½ pineapple and then press it through a sieve. Make up to 120ml/4 fl oz with water if necessary.

Watchpoint
Cornflour can be used to thicken many sauces, but always stir it in gradually, so that the sauce does not thicken too much.

TOMATO BEEF STIR-FRY

East meets West in a dish that is lightning-fast to cook
and tastes like a barbecue sauce stir-fry.

SERVES 4

460g/1lb sirloin or rump steak
Oil for frying
1 small red pepper, sliced
1 small green pepper, sliced
60g/2oz baby corn cobs
4 spring onions, shredded

Marinade
2 cloves garlic, crushed
90ml/6 tbsps wine vinegar
90ml/6 tbsps oil
Pinch of sugar, salt and pepper
1 bay leaf
1 tbsp ground cumin

Tomato Sauce
60ml/4 tbsps oil
1 medium onion, finely chopped
1-2 green chillies, finely chopped
1-2 cloves garlic, crushed
8 fresh ripe tomatoes, skinned, seeded and chopped
6 sprigs fresh coriander
3 tbsps tomato purée

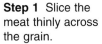

Step 1 Slice the meat thinly across the grain.

Step 3 Add the remaining ingredients to the wok and enough sauce to coat all ingredients thoroughly.

1. Slice the meat thinly across the grain. Combine in a plastic bag with the marinade ingredients. Tie the bag and toss the ingredients inside to coat. Place in a bowl and leave about 4 hours.

2. Heat the oil for the tomato sauce in a saucepan and cook the onion, chillies and garlic to soften but not brown. Add the remaining sauce ingredients and cook for about 15 minutes over a gentle heat. Purée in a food processor until smooth.

3. Heat a wok and add the meat in three batches, discarding the marinade. Cook to brown and set aside. Add about 2 tbsps of oil and cook the peppers for about 2 minutes. Add the corn and spring onions and return the meat to the wok. Cook for a further 1 minute and add the sauce. Cook to heat through and serve immediately.

Cook's Notes

Time
Preparation takes about 25 minutes, with 4 hours for marinating the meat. The sauce takes about 15 minutes to cook and the remaining ingredients need about 6-7 minutes.

Cook's Tip
Slicing the meat across the grain helps to keep it tender.

Preparation
The sauce may be prepared ahead of time and kept in the refrigerator for several days. It may also be frozen. Defrost the sauce at room temperature and then boil rapidly to reduce it again slightly.

BEEF IN OYSTER SAUCE

In this dish, sake is added to the marinade as it helps to tenderise the meat.

SERVES 4

1 tbsp sake
½ tsp bicarbonate of soda
½ tsp sugar
460g/1lb fillet steak, cut into thin slices
2 tbsps oil
1 spring onion, chopped
½ tsp chopped garlic
½ tsp chopped fresh root ginger
1 tbsp green peppercorns
2 tbsps oyster sauce
280ml/½ pint beef stock
Salt and pepper
1 tsp cornflour, combined with a little water

1. Mix together the sake, bicarbonate of soda and the sugar. Place the sliced meat in the marinade and marinate at room temperature for 1 hour.

2. When the meat is ready to cook, heat the oil in a wok and briefly stir-fry the spring onion, garlic, ginger and peppercorns.

3. Drain the meat, reserving the marinade. Add the drained meat to the wok, stir well and cook for 1 minute. Pour off any excess oil.

4. Pour the marinade over the beef and stir in the oyster sauce and the stock. Season well with salt and pepper.

5. Allow the sauce to reduce slightly. If it is still too thin, add a little of the cornflour, stirring continuously until the required consistency is reached.

Step 3 Add the drained meat to the wok and stir-fry for 1 minute.

Step 4 Add the marinade, oyster sauce and stock to the beef and season well.

Cook's Notes

Time
Preparation takes about 20 minutes, plus 1 hour marinating. Cooking takes about 15 minutes.

Cook's Tip
This dish should be cooked fairly rapidly, so that the meat does not dry out.

Variation
If green peppercorns are not available, use the mixed variety, but reduce the quantity by half.

BEEF WITH PINEAPPLE AND PEPPERS

This delicious sweet and sour main course makes a change from the more common pork version.

SERVES 4

460g/1lb fillet or rump steak
1 small pineapple
1 green pepper
1 red pepper
1 tbsp peanut oil
1 onion, roughly chopped
2 cloves garlic, crushed
2.5cm/1-inch fresh root ginger, peeled and thinly sliced
1 tsp sesame oil
2 tbsps light soy sauce
1 tbsp dark soy sauce
1 tsp sugar
1 tbsp brown sauce
60ml/4 tbsps water
Salt and freshly ground black pepper

Step 5 Stir-fry the beef and peppers with the onion in the wok.

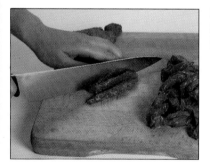

Step 1 Using a sharp knife, cut the steak into thin strips.

1. Using a sharp knife, cut the steak into thin strips across the grain.

2. Carefully peel the pineapple and cut out any eyes using a sharp knife or potato peeler. Cut the pineapple into slices and chop them into bite-sized pieces, removing the hard core.

3. Slice the green and red peppers in half. Remove and discard the cores and seeds. Chop the pepper flesh into thin strips.

4. Heat the peanut oil in a wok, and gently fry the onion, garlic and ginger, stirring continuously until the onion has softened slightly.

5. Add the strips of beef and pepper and continue stir-frying for 3 minutes.

6. Add the pineapple and stir-fry again for 2 minutes.

7. Remove the meat, vegetables and fruit from the wok and set aside on a plate.

8. Stir the sesame oil into the juices in the wok and add the soy sauces, sugar, brown sauce and water. Simmer rapidly for 30 seconds to reduce and thicken.

9. Stir the fruit, vegetables and beef back into the sauce. Season, heat through and serve immediately.

Cook's Notes

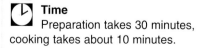

Time
Preparation takes 30 minutes, cooking takes about 10 minutes.

Watchpoint
Take care not to overcook the meat and vegetables, as this will greatly reduce the vitamin content of this dish.

Serving Idea
Serve with spring rolls and plain boiled rice.

STIR-FRIED CALVES' LIVER WITH PEPPERS AND CARROTS

Calves' liver is more expensive than other types of liver, but is so delicious and nutritious that it should be used more frequently.

SERVES 4

2 tbsps olive oil
1 onion, thinly sliced
1 clove garlic, thinly sliced
570g/1¼lbs calves' liver, cut into thin strips
2 tbsps seasoned wholemeal flour
60ml/4 tbsps dry sherry
140ml/¼ pint water, or vegetable stock
1 green pepper, cut into thin strips
3 large carrots, cut into strips
Salt and pepper
120g/4oz canned bean sprouts

1. Heat the olive oil in a large wok. Add the onion and garlic and stir-fry for 3 minutes.

2. Roll the strips of liver in the seasoned flour and add them to the wok, along with the onion. Stir-fry quickly, until the liver is sealed on the outside, but is still pink in the centre.

3. Stir the sherry into the liver and bring to a rapid boil. Add the water or stock to the liver, along with the green pepper, carrots and seasoning to taste.

4. Stir-fry the liver in the sauce for 3 minutes over a high heat.

Step 2 Roll the strips of calves' liver in the seasoned flour until they are evenly coated on all sides.

5. Add the bean sprouts to the wok and stir-fry for 1 minute, or just long enough to heat the bean sprouts through without cooking them.

Step 5 Stir the bean sprouts into the liver mixture and heat through for about 1 minute until they are warm, but still crunchy.

Cook's Notes

Time
Preparation takes 15-20 minutes and cooking takes 10-12 minutes.

Variation
Use lambs' liver for a stronger flavour.

Serving Idea
Serve with a bowl of brown rice and a tasty tomato salad.

PEKING BEEF

In China, meat is often simmered in large earthenware casseroles placed on asbestos mats. A wok is a convenient substitute and the stand does the work of the traditional mat.

SERVES 8

900g/2lb joint of beef
420ml/¾ pint white wine
570ml/1 pint water
4 whole spring onions, trimmed
2.5cm/1-inch piece fresh root ginger
3 star anise
140ml/¼ pint soy sauce
2 tsps sugar
1 carrot, peeled
2 sticks celery
½ mooli (daikon) radish, peeled

1. Place the beef in a wok and add the white wine, water, half the spring onions, the ginger and anise. Cover and simmer for about 1 hour.

2. Add the soy sauce and sugar, stir and simmer for 30 minutes longer, or until the beef is tender. Allow to cool in the liquid.

3. Shred the carrot, celery, mooli and remaining spring onions finely. Blanch them all, except the spring onion, in boiling water for about 1 minute. Rinse under cold water, drain and leave to dry.

4. When the meat is cold, remove it from the liquid and

Step 3 Cut the vegetables into 7.5cm/3-inch lengths. To shred carrots, cut each length into thin slices, stack the slices and cut through into thin strips.

Step 3 Cut the celery into three strips and then into thin strips.

cut into thin slices. Arrange on a serving plate and strain the liquid over it. Scatter over the shredded vegetables and serve cold.

Cook's Notes

Time
Preparation takes about 25 minutes if shredding the vegetables by hand. This can also be done with the fine shredding blade of a food processor. Cooking takes about 1½ hours.

Cook's Tip
If using a rolled roast, remove as much of the fat from the outside as possible. Skim off any fat that rises to the surface of the liquid as it cools, before pouring over the meat to serve.

Economy
Because of the long cooking time, less expensive cuts of meat are ideal for this dish.

BEEF WITH BROCCOLI

A slightly hot sauce accompanies this dish of beef and broccoli.

SERVES 4

680g/1½lbs rib of beef
225g/8oz broccoli
1 tbsp oil
2.5cm/1-inch piece fresh root ginger, peeled and finely
    chopped
1 tbsp sake
2 tsps chilli sauce
340ml/12 fl oz beef stock
2 tbsps dark soy sauce
Salt and pepper
1 tsp cornflour, combined with a little water

1. Cut the beef into small cubes. Do not remove any fat from the meat. Cut off the hard stem from the broccoli and separate the florets.

2. Bring a large quantity of salted water to the boil. Add the broccoli florets and cook until tender but still slightly crisp. Rinse immediately under cold water to stop the cooking process and then leave to drain.

3. Heat the oil in a wok and stir-fry the ginger and the meat. Pour off any excess fat and deglaze the wok with

Step 3 Add the chilli sauce, stock, and soy sauce to the wok and cook over a gentle heat for 10 minutes.

the sake. Stir in the chilli sauce, beef stock and the soy sauce. Cook over a gentle heat for 10 minutes.

4. Remove the meat with a slotted spoon and keep warm. Season the sauce with salt and pepper to taste.

5. Add the well-drained broccoli to the wok, allowing it to heat through completely. Remove with a slotted spoon and keep warm with the meat.

6. Add the cornflour to the sauce in the wok, stirring continuously until the required consistency is reached. Serve the meat and broccoli topped with the sauce.

Step 3 Add the sake to the wok and deglaze.

Step 5 Add the broccoli to the wok and heat through.

Cook's Notes

Time
Preparation takes about 20 minutes and cooking takes about 25 minutes.

Cook's Tip
If you prefer more sauce, add a little more beef stock before you thicken it with the cornflour.

Variation
Replace the broccoli with cauliflower florets.

SHREDDED BEEF WITH VEGETABLES

Stir-fried food is recognised as being nutritious and wholesome.
This classic dish is no exception, and has the bonus of being extremely
quick and easy to prepare.

SERVES 4

225g/8oz lean beef steak, cut into thin strips
½ tsp salt
60ml/4 tbsps vegetable oil
1 red and 1 green chilli, halved, seeded and sliced
  into strips
1 tsp vinegar
1 stick celery, cut into thin 5cm/2-inch strips
2 carrots, cut into thin 5cm/2-inch strips
1 leek, white part only, sliced into thin 5cm/2-inch
  strips
2 cloves garlic, finely chopped
1 tsp light soy sauce
1 tsp dark soy sauce
2 tsps Chinese wine, or dry sherry
1 tsp caster sugar
½ tsp freshly ground black pepper

1. Put the strips of beef into a large bowl and sprinkle with the salt. Rub the salt into the meat and allow to stand for 5 minutes.

2. Heat 1 tbsp of the oil in a large wok. When the oil begins to smoke, reduce the heat and stir in the beef and the chillies. Stir-fry for 4-5 minutes.

3. Add the remaining oil and continue stir-frying the beef until it turns crispy.

4. Add the vinegar and stir until it evaporates, then add the celery, carrots, leek and garlic. Stir-fry for 2 minutes.

5. Mix together the soy sauces, wine or sherry, sugar and pepper. Pour this mixture over the beef and cook for 2 minutes. Serve immediately.

Step 1 Put the finely sliced beef into a large bowl. Rub well with the salt and leave to stand.

Step 3 Add the remaining oil to the wok and continue stir-frying the beef until it is crisp.

Step 5 Pour the soy sauce mixture over the beef and stir-fry rapidly for about 2 minutes.

Cook's Notes

Time
Preparation takes about 15 minutes and cooking takes about 10 minutes.

Variation
Use your favourite combination of vegetables in place of those suggested in the recipe.

Serving Idea
Serve with plain boiled rice and prawn crackers.

SPICED BEEF

Fragrant and spicy, this delicious dish is quick and easy to make.
SERVES 4

460g/1lb fillet of beef
1 tsp soft brown sugar
2-3 star anise, ground
½ tsp ground fennel
1 tbsp dark soy sauce
2.5cm/1-inch piece fresh root ginger, grated
½ tsp salt
2 tbsps vegetable oil
6 spring onions, sliced
1 tbsp light soy sauce
½ tsp freshly ground black pepper

1. Cut the beef into thin strips about 2.5cm/1-inch long.

2. In a bowl, mix together the sugar, spices and dark soy sauce.

3. Put the beef, ginger and salt into the soy sauce mixture and stir well to coat evenly. Cover and allow to

Step 1 Cut the beef into thin strips about 2.5cm/1-inch long.

Step 3 Put the sliced beef, ginger and salt into the marinade and stir well to coat evenly.

Step 5 Stir-fry the beef with the spring onions for 4 minutes.

stand for 20 minutes.

4. Heat the oil in a wok and stir-fry the spring onions quickly for 1 minute.

5. Add the beef and fry, stirring constantly, for 4 minutes, or until the meat is well browned.

6. Stir in the light soy sauce and black pepper and cook gently for a further minute.

Cook's Notes

Time
Preparation takes about 30 minutes and cooking takes 5-6 minutes.

Variation
Add 120g/4oz sliced button mushrooms and 225g/8oz cooked Chinese egg noodles.

Serving Idea
Serve with a spicy dip.

BEEF WITH ONIONS

Lightly caramelised onions add a sweet note to this rich dish.

SERVES 4

460g/1lb fillet steak

Marinade
1 tbsp oil
1 tsp sesame oil
1 tbsp Chinese rice wine

1 tbsp oil
1 piece fresh root ginger, peeled and roughly chopped
3 onions, finely sliced
1 clove garlic, chopped
280ml/½ pint beef stock
Pinch of sugar
2 tbsps dark soy sauce
1 tsp cornflour, combined with a little water
Salt and pepper

1. Cut the fillet steak into very thin slices across the grain, using a sharp knife.

2. Mix together the marinade ingredients and stir in the meat. Leave to marinate for 30 minutes.

3. Heat the oil in a wok and stir-fry the ginger, onions and garlic until lightly browned.

4. Lift the meat out of the marinade with a slotted spoon and discard the marinade. Add the meat to the wok and stir-fry with the vegetables.

Step 5 Add the stock, soy and sugar to the wok and cook for 4 minutes.

5. Pour over the stock, sugar and soy sauce. Cook for 4 minutes.

6. Thicken the sauce with the cornflour mixture, stirring continuously until the required consistency is reached. Season with salt and pepper and serve immediately.

Step 6 Add the cornflour to the wok and stir continuously until thickened.

Cook's Notes

Time
Preparation takes about 15 minutes, plus 30 marinating. Cooking takes about 20 minutes.

Serving Idea
Serve this dish on a bed of boiled or steamed white rice.

Watchpoint
Keep a careful watch on the onions, and keep stirring, to make sure they don't burn.

LAMB WITH TRANSPARENT NOODLES

Transparent noodles, also known as cellophane noodles,
are made from mung bean flour.

SERVES 4

460g/1lb lean lamb
120g/4oz transparent noodles
2 tbsps oil
1 tsp chopped garlic
1 spring onion, chopped
2 tbsps soy sauce
200ml/7 fl oz lamb stock
Salt and pepper

1. Cut the meat into thin slices across the grain, using a sharp knife.

2. Bring a large quantity of salted water to the boil. Add the noodles and cook them for 45 seconds. Rinse immediately in cold water and set aside to drain.

3. Heat the oil in a wok and stir-fry the garlic and spring

Step 4 Stir in the soy sauce and the stock.

onion. Add the meat slices and stir-fry for 1 minute.

4. Stir in the soy sauce and the stock and cook over a gentle heat until the meat is cooked through.

5. Add the well-drained noodles, season to taste and allow to heat through. Serve hot.

Step 3 Add the sliced lamb to the wok and stir-fry for 1 minute.

Step 5 Add the noodles to the wok and heat through.

Cook's Notes

Time
Preparation takes about 10 minutes and cooking takes about 10 minutes.

Watchpoint
Once the stock has been added to the wok, reduce the heat and finish cooking very slowly so that the stock does not evaporate.

Serving Idea
Serve with steamed or lightly boiled mange tout.

STIR-FRIED LAMB WITH SESAME SEEDS

Lightly caramelized lamb with onions and sesame seeds makes an unusual stir-fry dish.

SERVES 4

745g/1lb 6oz shoulder of lamb, boned
2 tbsps oil
2 onions, thinly sliced
½ clove garlic, chopped
120ml/4 fl oz lamb stock or other meat stock
1 tsp sugar
1 tbsp soy sauce
½ tsp wine vinegar
Salt and pepper
1 tbsp sesame seeds

1. Cut away any excess fat from the lamb. Slice the meat very thinly using a sharp knife. Heat the oil in a wok and stir-fry the lamb. Remove when cooked and set aside.

2. In the same oil, fry the onions and garlic. Once they have become transparent, remove them and set aside.

3. Pour off any excess fat and put the meat back in the wok with the stock, sugar, soy sauce and vinegar. Continue cooking until the sauce is reduced. Season to taste with salt and pepper.

4. When the meat is lightly caramelized, sprinkle over

Step 1 Cut away any excess fat from the lamb.

Step 1 Slice the lamb thinly across the grain.

the sesame seeds and stir. Serve hot on a bed of the sautéed onions.

Cook's Notes

Time
Preparation takes about 10 minutes and cooking takes about 20 minutes.

Cook's Tip
Use any cut of lamb, cutting away any excess fat, before slicing very thinly.

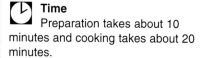

Preparation
This recipe is served without sauce. As the meat is caramelized, it should stay moist.

KIDNEYS WITH BACON

Stir-frying is an excellent way of cooking kidneys, as the brief cooking ensures that they do not become tough.

SERVES 4

460g/1lb lambs' kidneys
3 tbsps sherry
2 tbsps vegetable oil
8 rashers lean bacon, cut into 2.5cm/1-inch strips
1 onion, chopped
3 cloves garlic, crushed
1 tbsp tomato chutney
1 tbsp light soy sauce
2 tbsps water
Salt and freshly ground black pepper
1 tbsp cornflour
1½ tbsps fresh chopped parsley

Step 2 Cut a lattice design on the backs of each kidney, using a sharp knife, and taking care not to cut right through.

Step 1 Remove the hard core from each kidney half using a sharp knife or a small pair of scissors.

1. Trim any fat from the kidneys and cut each kidney in half with a sharp knife. Carefully trim out the hard core from the centre of each kidney with a sharp knife or scissors.

2. Cut a lattice design on the back of each kidney using a sharp knife and taking care not to cut right through. Put the kidneys into a bowl and stir in the sherry. Set aside for 15 minutes to marinate.

3. Heat the oil in a large wok and fry the bacon, onion and garlic for 5 minutes, stirring continuously to prevent burning. Remove from the wok and set aside on a plate.

4. Drain the kidneys and reserve the sherry marinade. Add the kidneys to the wok and stir-fry for 3 minutes only.

5. Stir the tomato chutney, soy sauce and water into the wok with the kidneys, then add the bacon and onion mixture. Season with salt and pepper and stir-fry gently for 5 minutes.

6. Blend the cornflour with the sherry marinade. Add 1 tbsp of the parsley to the cornflour mixture and stir this into the kidneys in the wok, mixing well until the sauce is thickened and smooth. Serve at once, sprinkled with the remaining parsley.

Step 4 Stir-fry the kidneys until they are completely browned.

Cook's Notes

Time
Preparation takes 20 minutes, cooking takes 25 minutes.

Cook's Tip
Do not cook the kidneys too quickly. Stir-fry them over a medium heat.

Serving Idea
Serve with rice or creamed potatoes.

Chapter 5
Rice, Noodles & Vegetables

Fried Rice • Prawn Egg Rice • Noodles with Peppers and Ginger

Shanghai Noodles • Spicy Oriental Noodles • Mee Goreng

Noodles with Ginger and Oyster Sauce

Aubergines and Peppers Szechuan Style • Stir-Fried Salad

Mushroom Stew • Ginger Cauliflower • Special Mixed Vegetables

Stir-Fried Chinese Leaves • Stir-Fried Tofu Salad

Vegetable Chop Suey • Stir-Fried Vegetables with Herbs

FRIED RICE

This basic recipe for a traditional Chinese accompaniment can be made more substantial with the addition of meat, poultry or seafood.

SERVES 6-8

3 tbsps oil
1 egg, beaten
1 tbsp soy sauce
460g/1lb cooked rice, well drained and dried
60g/2oz cooked peas
Salt and pepper
Dash of sesame oil
2 spring onions, thinly sliced

Step 2 Stir to coat the rice with the egg and toss the mixture over the heat to separate the grains of rice.

Step 2 Add the rice and peas on top of the egg mixture.

1. Heat a wok and add the oil. Pour in the egg and soy sauce, stir and cook until just beginning to set.

2. Add the rice and peas and stir to coat with the egg mixture. Allow to cook for about 3 minutes, stirring continuously. Add some seasoning to taste and the sesame oil.

3. Spoon into a serving dish and sprinkle over the spring onions.

Cook's Notes

Time
Preparation takes about 10 minutes and cooking takes about 4 minutes.

Variation
Cooked chicken, pork, crab or prawns may be added to the rice along with the peas.

Cook's Tip
Allow at least 20 minutes for the cooked rice to drain as dry as possible. Spread it out on a clean tea-towel to absorb all the excess moisture.

PRAWN EGG RICE

Serve this on its own for a tasty lunch or supper dish, or
as part of a more elaborate Chinese meal.

SERVES 6

460g/1lb long grain rice
2 eggs
½ tsp salt
60ml/4 tbsps oil
2 spring onions, chopped
1 large onion, chopped
2 cloves garlic, chopped
120g/4oz peeled prawns
60g/2oz shelled peas
2 tbsps dark soy sauce

1. Wash the rice thoroughly and put it in a saucepan. Add enough water to come 2.5cm/1 inch above the top of the rice.

2. Bring the rice to the boil, stir once, then reduce the heat. Cover and simmer the rice for 12-15 minutes, or until the liquid has been absorbed and the rice is just cooked.

3. Rinse the rice in cold water and fluff up with a fork, to separate the grains.

4. Beat the eggs with a pinch of the salt. Heat 1 tablespoon of the oil in a wok and cook both types of onions until soft, but not brown. Pour in the egg and stir gently, until the mixture sets. Remove the egg mixture and set it aside.

5. Heat another tablespoon of the oil and briskly fry the

Step 3 Rinse the rice in cold water and separate the grains with a fork.

Step 4 Gently cook the eggs with both types of onion until set and softly scrambled.

garlic, prawns and peas for 2 minutes. Remove from the wok and set aside.

6. Heat the remaining oil in the wok and stir in the rice and remaining salt. Stir-fry, to heat the rice through, then add the egg and the prawn mixtures and the soy sauce, stirring to blend thoroughly. Serve immediately.

Cook's Notes

Time
Preparation takes about 20 minutes and cooking takes about 15 minutes.

Variation
Use chopped red peppers or sweetcorn kernels, instead of the peas.

Freezing
Rice can be cooked and then frozen for up to 6 weeks. Frozen rice should be defrosted and rinsed before being used in this dish.

NOODLES WITH PEPPERS AND GINGER

Very thin strips of red and green pepper add colour and
interest to this noodle dish.

SERVES 4

1 red pepper
1 green pepper
225g/8oz Chinese noodles
1 tbsp oil
1 tsp each of chopped fresh root ginger and garlic
Salt and pepper

1. Cut the tops and bottoms off each pepper. Remove
the seeds and core, then slit the peppers up one side
and open them out flat. Cut each into three sections.

Step 2 Slice each section of pepper in half, horizontally.

Step 2 Cut the thin sections of pepper into very fine matchsticks.

2. Slice each section in half, horizontally, to make 12
very thin sections, then cut into very thin matchsticks.

3. Cook the noodles in boiling, lightly salted water,
stirring occasionally so that they do not stick.

4. Drain the noodles in a sieve and pass under cold
running water. Set aside to drain.

5. Heat the oil in a wok and stir-fry the peppers, ginger
and garlic for 1 minute, stirring continuously.

6. Add the well-drained noodles and stir-fry until the
noodles are hot. Season to taste and serve immediately.

Cook's Notes

Time
Preparation takes about 15
minutes and cooking takes about 10
minutes.

Watchpoint
If the noodles stick together, run
them under hot water until they
separate, then drain off the water and
continue with Step 6.

SHANGHAI NOODLES

In general, noodles are more popular in northern and eastern China, where wheat is grown, than in other parts of the country. Noodles make a popular snack in Chinese teahouses.

SERVES 4

120g/4oz chicken breasts
3 tbsps oil
460g/1lb thick Shanghai noodles
120g/4oz Chinese leaves
4 spring onions, thinly sliced
2 tbsps soy sauce
Freshly ground black pepper
Dash of sesame oil

1. Cut the chicken into thin strips across the grain, using a sharp knife. Heat the oil in a wok, add the chicken and stir-fry for 2-3 minutes.

2. Meanwhile, cook the noodles in boiling, salted water until just tender, about 6-8 minutes. Drain in a colander and rinse under hot water. Toss in the colander to drain and leave to dry.

Step 3 Stack up the Chinese leaves and, using a large sharp knife, cut across into thin strips.

3. Shred the Chinese leaves crossways into thin strips, and thinly slice the spring onions.

4. Add the shredded Chinese leaves and spring onions to the chicken in the wok along with the soy sauce, pepper and sesame oil. Cook for about 1 minute and toss in the cooked noodles. Stir well and heat through. Serve immediately.

Step 1 Cut the chicken into thin strips across the grain.

Step 4 Add the cooked noodles, stir well and heat through.

Cook's Notes

Time
Preparation takes about 10 minutes, cooking takes 6-8 minutes.

Variation
Pork may be used instead of the chicken. Add shredded fresh spinach, if wished and cook with the Chinese leaves.

Buying Guide
Shanghai noodles are fresh egg Chinese noodles which are available in Oriental supermarkets and also some delicatessens. If unavailable, substitute dried Chinese noodles.

SPICY ORIENTAL NOODLES

A most versatile vegetable dish, this goes well with meat
or stands alone as a vegetarian main course.

SERVES 4

225g/8oz Chinese noodles (medium thickness)
75ml/5 tbsps oil
4 carrots, peeled
225g/8oz broccoli
12 dried shiitake mushrooms, soaked in warm water
   for 30 minutes
1 clove garlic, peeled
4 spring onions, diagonally sliced
1-2 tsps chilli sauce, mild or hot
60ml/4 tbsps soy sauce
60ml/4 tbsps rice wine or dry sherry
2 tsps cornflour

1. Cook the noodles in boiling salted water for about 4-5 minutes. Drain well, rinse under hot water to remove the excess starch and drain again. Toss with about 1 tbsp of the oil, to prevent them sticking together.

2. Using a large, sharp knife, slice the carrots thinly on the diagonal.

3. Cut the florets off the stems of the broccoli and divide into even-sized but not too small sections. Slice the stalks thinly on the diagonal. If they seem tough, peel them before slicing.

4. Place the vegetables in boiling water for about 2 minutes to blanch. Drain and rinse under cold water to stop them cooking, and leave to drain dry.

5. Remove and discard the mushroom stems and slice the caps thinly. Set aside with the spring onions.

6. Heat a wok and add the remaining oil with the garlic clove. Leave the garlic in the pan while the oil heats and then remove it. Add the carrots and broccoli and stir-fry about 1 minute. Add mushrooms and spring onions and continue to stir-fry, tossing the vegetables in the pan continuously.

7. Combine the chilli sauce, soy sauce, wine and cornflour, mixing well. Pour over the vegetables and cook until the sauce clears. Toss with the noodles, heat them through and serve immediately.

Step 7 Cook the vegetables and sauce ingredients until the cornflour thickens and clears.

Cook's Notes

Time
Preparation takes about 25 minutes and cooking takes about 7-8 minutes.

Buying Guide
If dried shiitake mushrooms are unavailable, substitute fresh ordinary mushrooms and omit the soaking.

Serving Idea
Use hot or cold as a side dish with chicken, meat or fish, or serve as a starter.

MEE GORENG

These 'celebration stir-fry noodles' are of Indonesian origin and are so easy to prepare that they make an ideal quick lunch or supper dish.

SERVES 4

225g/8oz fine egg noodles
60ml/4 tbsps peanut oil
1 onion, finely chopped
2 cloves garlic, crushed
1 green chilli, seeded and finely sliced
1 tsp chilli paste
120g/4oz pork, finely sliced
2 sticks of celery, sliced
¼ small cabbage, finely shredded
Salt and pepper
1 tbsp light soy sauce
120g/4oz cooked peeled prawns

1. Soak the noodles in hot water for about 8 minutes until they are soft. Rinse in cold water and drain thoroughly in a colander.

2. Heat the oil in a wok and stir-fry the onion, garlic and chilli until the onion is soft and just golden brown.

3. Add the chilli paste and stir in well.

4. Add the pork, celery and cabbage to the fried onions and stir-fry for about 3 minutes, or until the pork is cooked through. Season to taste.

Step 1 Soak the noodles in hot water for about 8 minutes until they are soft. Rinse in cold water and drain thoroughly in a colander.

5. Stir in the soy sauce, noodles and prawns, tossing the mixture together thoroughly and heating through before serving.

Step 4 Stir-fry the pork, celery and cabbage with the onion mixture for 3 minutes, or until the pork is cooked through.

Cook's Notes

Time
Preparation takes about 20 minutes and cooking takes about 15 minutes.

Variation
Substitute sliced chicken breast for the pork.

Watchpoint
Great care should be taken when preparing chillies. Do not get any juice into the eyes or mouth. If this should happen, rinse well with lots of cold water.

NOODLES WITH GINGER AND OYSTER SAUCE

Adding a few vegetables and flavouring to ordinary
Chinese noodles transforms them into a really tasty dish.

SERVES 4

225g/8oz Chinese noodles
1 carrot
1 courgette
5cm/2-inch piece fresh root ginger
1 tbsp oil
1 spring onion, cut into thin rounds
1 tbsp soy sauce
2 tbsps oyster sauce
Salt and pepper

1. Cook the noodles in boiling, salted water, rinse under cold water and set aside to drain.

2. Cut the carrot into thin julienne strips. Thickly peel the courgette to include a little of the flesh and cut into thin julienne strips. Discard the centre of the courgette.

3. Peel one side of the fresh root ginger, removing any hard parts. Cut off three long thin slices using a potato peeler. Cut the slices into thin strips using a very sharp knife.

4. Heat the oil in a wok and stir-fry the spring onion for 10 seconds; add the carrot, courgette and ginger and stir-fry briefly. Stir in the noodles and cook for 1 minute.

5. Stir in the soy and oyster sauces and continue cooking until heated through. Season with salt and pepper and serve.

Step 3 Peel the ginger sparingly.

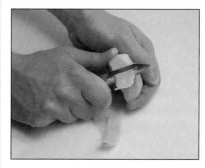

Step 3 Cut 3 thin slices from the ginger using a vegetable peeler.

Step 3 Cut the slices into fine shreds using a very sharp knife.

Cook's Notes

Time
Preparation takes about 15 minutes and cooking takes about 15 minutes.

Variation
Cook the noodles in chicken stock instead of salted water to give them extra flavour.

Watchpoint
Stir-fry the ginger and the other vegetables very quickly, to avoid browning them. Lower the heat if necessary.

AUBERGINES AND PEPPERS SZECHUAN STYLE

Authentic Szechuan food is fiery hot. Outside China, restaurants often tone down the taste for Western palates.

SERVES 4

1 large aubergine
Oil for cooking
2 cloves garlic, crushed
2.5cm/1-inch piece fresh root ginger, shredded
1 onion, cut into 2.5cm/1-inch pieces
1 small green pepper, cut into 2.5cm/1-inch pieces
1 small red pepper, cut into 2.5cm/1-inch pieces
1 red or green chilli, seeded and cut into thin strips
120ml/4 fl oz chicken or vegetable stock
1 tsp sugar
1 tsp vinegar
Pinch of salt and pepper
1 tsp cornflour
1 tbsp soy sauce
Dash of sesame oil

Step 1 Cut the aubergine in half and lightly score the cut surfaces.

Step 1 Sprinkle lightly with salt and leave on kitchen paper or in a colander to drain.

1. Cut the aubergine in half and lightly score the cut surfaces. Sprinkle lightly with salt and leave to drain in a colander or on kitchen paper for 30 minutes.

2. After 30 minutes, squeeze the aubergine gently to extract any bitter juices and rinse thoroughly under cold water. Pat dry and cut the aubergine into 2.5cm/1-inch cubes.

3. Heat about 3 tbsps oil in a wok. Add the aubergine and stir-fry for about 4-5 minutes. It may be necessary to add more oil as the aubergine cooks. Remove from the wok and set aside.

4. Reheat the wok and add 2 tbsps oil. Add the garlic and ginger and stir-fry for 1 minute. Add the onion and stir-fry for 2 minutes. Add the green pepper, red pepper and chilli and stir-fry for 1 minute. Return the aubergine to the wok along with the remaining ingredients.

5. Bring to the boil, stirring constantly, and cook until the sauce thickens and clears. Serve immediately.

Cook's Notes

Time
Preparation takes about 30 minutes, cooking takes about 7-8 minutes.

Cook's Tip
Lightly salting the aubergine will help draw out any bitter juices.

Serving Suggestions
Serve as a vegetarian stir-fry dish with plain or fried rice, or serve as a side dish.

STIR-FRIED SALAD

Vegetables prepared this way retain all of their crunchiness as they are cooked so quickly.

SERVES 4

1 onion
2 large leeks
3 tbsps olive oil
2 cloves garlic, crushed
225g/8oz mange tout peas, topped and tailed
120g/4oz bean sprouts
Salt and freshly ground black pepper
1 tbsp fresh, chopped coriander leaves

Step 1 Rinse the split leeks under running water, separating the leaves to wash out any grit or dirt.

1. Peel the onion and cut it into thin rings. Trim the leeks and cut down the length of one side. Open the leeks out and wash thoroughly under running water.

2. Cut each leek into three pieces, then thinly slice the pieces lengthways into thin strips.

3. Heat the oil in a large wok and add the onion and garlic. Cook for 2 minutes, stirring all the time until the

Step 2 Cut the pieces of leek lengthways into thin strips.

Step 1 Peel the onion and slice it into thin rings.

onion has softened but not browned.

4. Add the mange tout peas and sliced leeks to the wok and continue stir-frying for 4 minutes.

5. Add the bean sprouts, some seasoning and the chopped coriander and cook briskly for a further 2 minutes. Serve piping hot.

Cook's Notes

Time
Preparation takes 15 minutes, cooking takes about 10 minutes.

Cook's Tip
If using fresh bean sprouts, blanch them in boiling water for 1 minute, rinse in cold water and drain thoroughly before adding.

 Serving Idea
Serve this dish with rice, and sprinkle it liberally with soy sauce.

MUSHROOM STEW

Dried Chinese mushrooms, cooked with oyster sauce
and ginger, make a delicious vegetable side dish.

SERVES 4

225g/8oz dried Chinese black mushrooms
225g/8oz dried Chinese shiitake mushrooms
1 tbsp oil
1 tbsp each chopped garlic and fresh root ginger
280ml/½ pint chicken stock
1 tbsp oyster sauce
Salt and pepper

1. Soak both types of dried mushrooms in warm water for 15 minutes.

2. Transfer the mushrooms to a saucepan and cook in lightly salted, boiling water for 45 minutes. Rinse under cold water and set aside to drain.

3. Heat the oil in a wok and stir-fry the garlic and ginger. Add the mushrooms and stir-fry briefly.

4. Add the stock, followed by the oyster sauce and salt and pepper to taste. Continue cooking until the sauce thickens and coats the mushrooms.

Step 3 Add the boiled mushrooms to the wok and stir-fry briefly.

Step 4 Add the stock, oyster sauce and seasoning to the wok and cook until the sauce coats the mushrooms.

Cook's Notes

Time
Preparation takes 10 minutes and cooking takes about 1 hour.

Watchpoint
After removing the mushrooms from the cooking water, drain it through a fine strainer, so that any sand or grit is trapped in the strainer.

 Serving Idea
Just before serving, sprinkle over some freshly chopped parsley.

GINGER CAULIFLOWER

This is a very simple and extremely subtle vegetable dish,
deliciously spiced with ginger.

SERVES 4

3 tbsps oil
1 medium onion, chopped
2.5cm/1-inch piece fresh root ginger, peeled and
 sliced
1-2 green chillies, cut in half lengthways
1 medium cauliflower, cut into 2.5cm/1-inch florets
Salt to taste
2-3 sprigs fresh coriander leaves, chopped
Juice of 1 lemon

Step 2 Stir the cauliflower and salt into the fried onion mixture. Mix well to coat the cauliflower evenly in the oil.

Step 1 Heat the oil in a wok until it is hot, add the onion, ginger and chillies and stir-fry for 2-3 minutes.

1. Heat the oil in a wok, add the onion, ginger and chillies and stir-fry for 2-3 minutes.

2. Add the cauliflower and salt to taste. Stir to mix well. Cover and cook over a low heat for 5-6 minutes.

3. Add the chopped coriander leaves and cook for a further 2-3 minutes, or until the cauliflower florets are just tender.

4. Sprinkle with the lemon juice, mix in well and serve immediately.

Cook's Notes

Time
Preparation takes 15 minutes and cooking also takes about 15 minutes.

Cook's Tip
Leaving the chilli seeds in will produce a very hot dish. If a milder dish is required, remove the seeds from the chilli.

Watchpoint
Great care must be taken when preparing fresh chillies. Do not get any juice into eyes or mouth. If this should happen, rinse thoroughly with lots of cold water.

SPECIAL MIXED VEGETABLES

Use other varieties of vegetables for an equally colourful side dish.

SERVES 4

3 tomatoes
1 tbsp oil
1 clove garlic, crushed
2.5cm/1-inch piece fresh root ginger, sliced
4 leaves Chinese cabbage, shredded
60g/2oz flat mushrooms, thinly sliced
60g/2oz bamboo shoots, sliced
3 sticks celery, diagonally sliced
60g/2oz baby corn cobs, cut in half if large
1 small red pepper, thinly sliced
60g/2oz bean sprouts
2 tbsps light soy sauce
Dash of sesame oil
Salt and pepper

1. To skin the tomatoes, remove the stems and place in boiling water for 5 seconds.

2. Remove from the boiling water with a draining spoon and place in a bowl of cold water. Cut out the core end using a small sharp knife.

Step 2 Remove the tomatoes to cold water to stop them cooking. The skin will then peel away easily.

3. Cut the tomatoes in half and then in quarters. Use a teaspoon or a serrated edged knife to remove the seeds and cores.

4. Heat the oil in a wok and add the garlic and ginger. Stir-fry briefly then add all the vegetables, except the tomatoes, in the order given. Stir-fry for 2 minutes.

5. Stir in the soy sauce and sesame oil, season to taste and add the tomatoes. Heat through for 30 seconds and serve immediately.

Step 1 To skin the tomatoes, place them first in a pan of boiling water for 5 seconds.

Step 3 Cut into quarters and remove the seeds, core and juice with a teaspoon, or use a serrated edged knife.

Cook's Notes

Time
Preparation takes about 25 minutes, cooking takes about 2½-3 minutes.

Variation
Other vegetables such as broccoli florets, cauliflower florets, mange tout, courgettes or French beans may be used.

Serving Idea
This dish can also be served as a vegetarian main dish with plain or fried rice.

STIR-FRIED CHINESE LEAVES

Stir-fried Chinese leaves, courgettes and peppers, flavoured with
sesame oil and soy sauce makes a delicious, crisp-textured side dish.

SERVES 4

460g/1lb Chinese leaves
2 courgettes
2 tbsps oil
1 tsp chopped garlic
1 tbsp chopped red chillies
1 tbsp soy sauce
Salt and pepper
Few drops of sesame oil

Step 1 Cut the courgettes into julienne sticks.

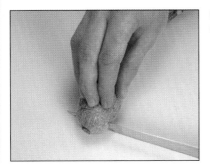

Step 1 Trim the courgettes.

1. Shred the Chinese leaves quite finely. Trim the courgettes, then cut them into julienne sticks.

2. Heat the oil in a wok, add the Chinese leaves and garlic and stir-fry for 2 minutes.

3. Add the courgettes, chopped red chilli, soy sauce and salt and pepper. Continue cooking for 3 minutes and serve hot with the sesame oil drizzled on top.

Cook's Notes

Time
Preparation takes about 10 minutes and cooking takes about 5 minutes.

Variation
Reduce the amount of chilli to suit your own taste.

Cook's Tip
Cooked in this way, the Chinese leaves will remain crisp.

STIR-FRIED TOFU SALAD

This recipe is ideal for vegetarians, but is so delicious
that it will be enjoyed by everyone.

SERVES 4-6

1 cake of tofu
120g/4oz mange tout peas
60g/2oz mushrooms
2 carrots, peeled
2 sticks celery
4 spring onions, trimmed
140ml/¼ pint vegetable oil
60g/2oz broccoli, in small florets
3 tbsps lemon juice
2 tsps honey
1 tsp grated fresh root ginger
3 tbsps soy sauce
Dash of sesame oil
60g/2oz unsalted roasted peanuts
120g/4oz canned bean sprouts, drained
½ head Chinese leaves

1. Drain the tofu well and press gently to remove any excess moisture. Cut into 1.25cm/½-inch cubes.

2. Trim the tops and tails from the mange tout peas and thinly slice the mushrooms with a sharp knife. Cut the carrots and celery into thin slices, on the diagonal. Slice the spring onions in the same way.

3. Heat 2 tbsps of the vegetable oil in a wok. Stir in the mange tout, mushrooms, celery, carrots and broccoli and cook for 2 minutes, stirring constantly. Remove the vegetables from the wok and set them aside to cool.

4. Put the remaining oil into a small bowl and whisk in the lemon juice, honey, grated ginger, soy sauce

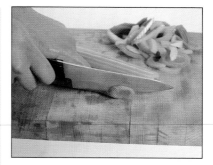

Step 2 Slice the carrots and celery thinly, cutting with your knife at an angle to produce diagonal pieces.

and sesame oil.

5. Stir the sliced spring onions, peanuts and bean sprouts into the cooled vegetables.

6. Mix the dressing into the salad vegetables, then add the tofu. Toss the tofu into the salad very carefully so that it does not break up.

7. Shred the Chinese leaves and arrange them on a serving platter. Pile the salad ingredients over the top and serve well chilled.

Step 6 Toss the tofu very carefully into the salad ingredients, taking care not to break it up.

Cook's Notes

Time
Preparation takes about 25 minutes, cooking takes 2-4 minutes.

Preparation
Make sure that the stir-fried vegetables are completely cool before adding the remaining salad ingredients, or they will lose their crispness.

Variation
Use shredded cooked chicken in place of the tofu in this recipe, for a meat version.

VEGETABLE CHOP SUEY

Serve this dish with extra soy sauce and plain boiled rice
for a filling vegetarian main course.

SERVES 4

1 green pepper
1 red pepper
1 carrot
½ cucumber
1 courgette, thickly peeled and the central core
   discarded
1 onion
2 cloves garlic
2 tbsps oil
2 tsps sugar
2 tbsps soy sauce
120ml/4 fl oz chicken stock
Salt and pepper

1. Cut the peppers, carrot, cucumber and courgette into thin julienne sticks.

2. Slice the onion into quarters, then cut into thin, even slices. Chop the garlic very finely.

3. Heat the oil in a wok and stir-fry the peppers and garlic for 30 seconds. Add the onion and carrot and stir-fry for another 30 seconds.

4. Add the cucumber and the courgette and cook for 1 minute, stirring and shaking the wok continuously.

Step 2 Cut the onion into quarters.

Step 2 Cut the onion into thin, even slices.

5. Stir in the sugar, soy sauce, chicken stock and salt and pepper, mixing together evenly. Simmer until all the ingredients are fully incorporated. Serve piping hot.

Cook's Notes

Time
Preparation takes about 15 minutes and cooking takes about 5 minutes.

Cook's Tip
If you follow the order given above for cooking the vegetables, they will all be cooked but still slightly crisp.

 Variation
You could add blanched bean sprouts or sliced, blanched bamboo shoots to this dish.

STIR-FRIED VEGETABLES WITH HERBS

Crisply cooked vegetables with plenty of chives make a perfect side dish, hot or cold.

SERVES 6

4 sticks celery
4 medium courgettes
2 red peppers
30-45ml/3-4 tbsps oil
Pinch of salt and pepper
1 tsp chopped fresh oregano or marjoram
60ml/4 tbsps snipped fresh chives

1. Slice the celery diagonally, into pieces about 1.25cm/½-inch thick.

2. Cut the courgettes in half lengthways and then cut into 1.25cm/½-inch thick slices.

3. Remove all the seeds and pith from the peppers and cut them into diagonal 2.5cm/1-inch pieces.

4. Heat the oil in a wok over a medium high heat. Add

Step 1 Cut the celery sticks into 1.25cm/½-inch slices using a large, sharp knife.

Step 3 Seed the peppers and cut them into strips. Cut the strips into 2.5cm/1-inch diagonal pieces.

Step 6 Stir-fry all the vegetables, seasonings and herbs until the vegetables are tender-crisp.

the celery and stir-fry until barely tender.

5. Add the courgettes and peppers and stir-fry until all the vegetables are tender-crisp.

6. Add the salt, pepper and oregano or marjoram and cook for 30 seconds more. Stir in the chives and serve immediately.

Cook's Notes

Time
Preparation takes about 25 minutes and cooking takes about 5 minutes.

Variation
Use other vegetables such as carrots or mushrooms and alter cooking times accordingly.

Serving Idea
Serve hot as an accompaniment to chicken, ham or with stuffed poussins. The vegetables may also be served cold as a salad with a dash of lemon or vinegar added.

Index